# THE CHOSEN ONE

# JEANNE KREMERS

*in appreciation and Gratitude*
*Jeanne Kremers*

# THE CHOSEN ONE

## FACING CANCER WITH GRACE AND EASE

**TATE PUBLISHING**
AND ENTERPRISES, LLC

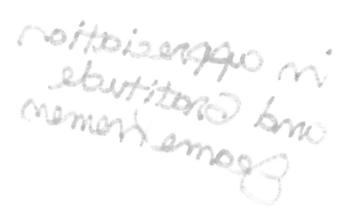

Published by Tate Publishing & Enterprises, LLC
127 E. Trade Center Terrace | Mustang, Oklahoma 73064 USA
1.888.361.9473 | www.tatepublishing.com

Tate Publishing is committed to excellence in the publishing industry. The company reflects the philosophy established by the founders, based on Psalm 68:11,
*"The Lord gave the word and great was the company of those who published it."*

Published in the United States of America

ISBN: 978-1-62510-439-7
1. Biography & Autobiography / Personal Memoirs
2. Health & Fitness / Diseases / Cancer
13.07.17

# DEDICATION

I would like to dedicate this book to all those who have fought and continue to fight this monster called cancer, and the loved ones who inspire them to continue to fight.

I dedicate this book to the greatest power within you, your perseverance to continue to fight on for your loved ones when you are tired of the fight for yourself.

# ACKNOWLEDGMENTS

Along the journey I have been blessed to have the support and guidance of so many great people. They have helped me dig deeper than I thought possible, giving me the valuable gift of gratitude and personal growth from the vulnerable experience.

Thank you from the bottom of my heart to my husband, Duane, and my two blessings, daughter, Kira, and son, Bradley. I am so grateful for you being at my side, supporting, guiding, and nursing me both physically and emotionally. Not a day goes by that I don't appreciate you. You are my passion for living.

A special thanks to Ashley Canfield and Robin Yorek for the tremendous support you gave to our children so they could spend quality time with family at such a difficult time.

My two sweet little blessings (grandchildren), my sweet little monkeyshine Kitana, my little nurse mate, and Mason (Gibby) my little man. I am so blessed to have you at my side; you are so healing and gratifying to me. You inspire me every day.

I express a great sense of gratitude and love to my beloved parents, Ann and Sylvester Oldakowski, and my nine siblings for their mutual support, strength, encouragement, and guidance. You have taught and influenced me in a way you will never know.

All individuals and teams involved in my care, such as general doctors, oncologists, radiologists, surgeons, plastic surgeons, and all other medical individuals, I want to express my deepest appreciation and gratitude to all you have done to assist in my care. Your individual fine-tuned skills and positive attitudes have inspired me. I could never express all the honor, praise, and gratitude you deserve. I am grateful for the diligence and dedication demonstrated by all of you and your teams.

A special thanks and appreciation go to my blessing, Peggy Lange. I am deeply indebted to you for all the assistance, encouragement, and support you supplied to me so I could focus on my health.

The tremendous outreach and support from the people at my place of work astonishes me. I am grateful for all who assisted me in the smooth transition back to my job.

Special friends: I extend my heartfelt gratification to those who have been at our sides day and night every step of the way. Thank you for the strong support of prayers, encouragement, and assistance. We are blessed to have people like you in our lives.

A heartfelt gratification goes to (my angel) Cassandra Woody and her special team at Tate Publishing for all their dedication, collaborative efforts, and highly skilled professionals who have given me the opportunity through their wisdom, encouragement, and dedication to be able to bring the readers this book.

A special thanks to Kira Yorek for the wonderful photography created for this book.

Foremost, I want to thank God for the inspiration, life experiences, and giftedness that led me to write this book; his handiwork is done through me.

# TABLE OF CONTENTS

# PROLOGUE:

# CANCER KNOWS
# NO LIMITS

*Cancer is nondiscriminatory. It knows no gender or race. It will take anyone. Safeguard your body and that of your children's.*

Before I begin with my own story, I want to talk about one of the scariest and most infuriating aspects of cancer, and that is that cancer is something that can happen to anyone at anytime, and it doesn't care what it might be interrupting. Cancer doesn't know that you are a mother or that you have a daughter about to get married, and it doesn't care that you have many more precious moments to experience. It can happen during pregnancy, to children, to young adults starting out new lives, and to parents and grandparents who are enjoying life, watching their loved ones grow around them. It's an unfair disease that no one should ever have to endure, but still many do.

*Kira (Daughter), Brad (Son), Myself,*
*Duane (Husband), and Edna (Mother in Law)*

I work in a hospital, so I see firsthand how cancer can touch anyone. It has always been upsetting for me to watch, but now that I've had so much personal experience, the loss of a cancer client heavily pulls at my heartstrings. At times, it feels so overwhelming and so utterly unfair that I can hardly handle it.

The aftermath of cancer never goes away. I have a special place in my heart for every cancer patient I come across and all of their families as well. It's a disease that keeps people locked in fear, and it steals so much joy. Because I know this about the illness, I have made a conscious decision to ask every day, *Do I have joy in my life? Have I brought joy into the lives of others?* These are two questions I try every day to live by. I attempt to enhance someone's life every day just for having known me. It costs nothing but my time and a loving, caring heart. And if it could bring just a little comfort to those who have also found out how cruel cancer is, I feel the time is well spent.

Although cancer is neither sexist nor racist and being susceptible to it is one thing that every person in every culture everywhere has in common, there are some things that we can do to help better prepare ourselves for it and to be sure that, even if we do have to fight for our lives against it, we can come out victors over this devastating illness. One of those things is genetic testing.

For my family, cancer was more a part of our family history than any of us realized until it reared its ugly head and forced us to see how deep its roots went into our family tree. Once a family member is diagnosed, though, genetic testing can be done to find out if the cancer is hereditary and if the cancer patient is a carrier of a certain gene that causes it. I have been proactive in this way and opted to do the testing.

Something else that I do to fight and that I hope gives others the courage to keep fighting is to participate in cancer walks. Even though there are times I know I may not be physically or emotionally prepared for the walks, I do them because I feel if they inspire just one person, I have done something great. I hear things on them sometimes that I am not emotionally ready to hear, but mentally I need to do the walks for my victory and to give power to women and men who could not walk for themselves.

At the end of each walk I do, I'm generally spent in every way one can be. During one in particular, one of my sisters lost a toe nail, the other had a couple of blisters, and we all got slightly sunburned, but we did it to speak out in our own way against the enemy called cancer. I sometimes find myself angry at the color *pink* and what it represents (cancer). Mostly I get angry at the word *cancer*. I've seen the pain in thousands of faces caused from cancer intruding into their lives and the lives of loved ones. But when I do these walks, I also feel a sense of gratitude for everyone there doing the same thing that I am.

It's not just breast cancer patients I'm walking for though; it's for every cancer patient and their families everywhere that I walk. It's to stand up against the mortal enemy that I walk. It's to take a little bit of power from the disease that I walk. This disease is nondiscriminatory, but that also means that people of all ages, races, backgrounds, and genders are rallying against it. The disease is nondiscriminatory, but so are the people fighting against it, and that is something powerful.

# CHAPTER ONE:

# THE THANK-YOU NOTE

Life is a strange thing. It's exciting, frightening, joyful, heartbreaking, infuriating, and above all else, life is absolutely unpredictable. In the last decade, I've learned the last part well. I've also learned that life doesn't always seem fair, but we can't let that aspect of it steal our gratitude for all the amazing parts that life offers us.

Ironically, I learned how vital gratitude is the day I found out that there might be a fourth cancer diagnosis in my immediate family. That's right, fourth. My dad had already passed from cancer, one sister was diagnosed just after my father, and I was diagnosed a year later, only to hear that another sister had a mammogram come back questionable. I couldn't help but think that this was how Dad must have felt.

When something so extreme happens, and keeps happening, you either get very bitter or you start to reevaluate and do some soul-searching to find out how it is you are supposed to handle so much. I decided to do the latter, but I needed God to help.

Cancer is tough, really tough. It takes you through so many different stages. It seems like once you're diagnosed, it's just one thing after the next that you have to learn to cope with. One of the major things is chemotherapy, since chemo does so much to your body and to your appearance. Luckily they have classes to help cancer patients get through the chemo changes, and they also allow each patient to bring a loved one for support.

When I decided I'd go to the classes to learn to live with the new me, I asked my youngest sister, Kelly, to accompany me. I didn't realize when I asked her to go that I'd need her for more than just moral support to get through a class on how to deal with my ever-changing physical appearance.

The day of my first class arrived, and I got in my car and headed for Kelly's house to pick her up. She lived about half an hour from me, so I had some time to think and reflect on everything. I did my best to keep a positive outlook about the whole thing. I tried to listen to upbeat music and think of funny little jokes I could make to lighten the situation for both my sister and me. I thought I might as well make the best of all this, and part of making the best of it was allowing myself to laugh.

Then my phone started to vibrate in my purse. I looked at the screen and saw that it was my middle sister, Mary. What she was about to say was going to thrash through all the good vibes and positive thoughts I was trying to generate that day.

"Hi, Jeanne. It's Mary," she started, and there was something in her voice that told me she wasn't call-

THE CHOSEN ONE    19

ing with good news. "So I had my mammogram, and they're a little concerned about the results," she explained. "There are some lumps."

That put me over the edge. Every thought, feeling, and emotion I had was washed out by panic. This could not be happening, not again. Positivity and light-heartedness weren't even on the radar anymore. All I had left was fear and anger. No family deserved this, especially not mine, I thought. How could God let so much happen at one time?

I didn't want to be mad, not at God, but I didn't get what was happening. There was just no explanation for so much heartache. I knew that being angry wasn't going to get me far, though, so instead I began to pray. All the way to pick up my sister I prayed to God and I cried.

"God, please, promise me you're not gonna take one of my sisters." I sobbed, clenching the steering wheel as I tried to see past my tears. "You gotta promise me! What are you doing to us? Why are you taking my family? What do I need to learn from this? What can I change to make it stop?"

I was hysterical. My heart throbbed, and my head felt like it was swelling as I pleaded with God. I didn't hold anything back. It was me and God in that car, and I just put it all out for him to see. I was obviously not getting something, and I laid it all out that day. If God would just show me something, anything, to lead me in some direction, I'd do it. I needed him more than ever to give some sort of explanation.

"Please, can you just protect my family?" I wailed as I wiped the never-ending tears that streamed down my face. "Please don't take any more of my family." I needed God to hear me. I needed him to really listen and to answer.

All of a sudden, I heard this voice that must've been in my head, but it was almost like somebody was sitting next to me saying it. It wasn't my voice; it was a man's voice.

"I promise not to take any more of your sisters, but you have to do one thing for me," the voice said.

"Anything," I replied, out loud. "Anything, just don't take any more of my sisters. This is horrible. I don't think we can live through another family death."

"You have to do one thing for me, and your sisters are safe."

"Anything," I pleaded.

"You have to write a thank-you note," the voice told me.

*A thank you note?* I thought. *I can do that.* And do that I did. I started listing off anybody who brought any food, anybody who visited or sent flowers or a card. Anyone who had done anything at all, I made a list to write them a thank-you note. I wrote their names down and put them in a special spot so I would be sure that everyone received a thank you from me.

"Hopefully I didn't forget anybody," I said after listing everyone I could think of. "I think I got everybody, though."

"You did forget somebody," the voice replied.

"I did?" I asked. "Who?"

I wanted to be sure I had done my end of the deal, and I also wanted everyone to know how much he or she meant to me. I didn't want anyone to feel left out or to have anyone's thoughtfulness go unnoticed.

Then he said, "You forgot me. You forgot God."

He was right; I did forget him. I forgot all about him. In all this mess, I forgot God, so I said, "I promise you I will write you a thank-you note."

So we finished class at around eight thirty or nine that night. I had done chemo earlier that day at 3:00 p.m., and I still hadn't gone to the bathroom, which was important because the chemo could burn your bladder if you didn't, so I was gulping down water at this point trying to go. I felt horrible, so I knew I needed to do something to get the junk out of my body.

"Kelly, do you know I haven't voided since chemo class," I said, a little concerned about it.

"Let's try some lemon water," Kelly suggested, so I tried some lemon water at Kelly's and then again at home, but midnight came and still nothing. I had about fourteen glasses of water on board, and it was starting to get difficult breathing. I couldn't lie down anymore because all the fluid was starting to get in between my tissues; my body was very puffy. I couldn't think of anything else to do, so I had another lemon water, and finally the pressure released, but it was 3:00 a.m. by this point.

So there I was, up at three o'clock in the morning in a silent house with only my thoughts. *I need to write the thank-you note*, I thought as I sat in the living room that was completely quiet. I got up, grabbed my notebook, and I thought, *Okay, I need to write a letter to God.*

I moved to the dining room table, and there I sat, pen in hand, staring down at the blank paper. Nothing was coming. And the harder I tried, the less I could think to write. What kind of thank-you note do you write to God? How do I begin to thank God for what I was going through? I didn't even know where to begin.

As I sat there all alone in the dining room with college-ruled paper taunting me, I thought, *What can I possibly thank you for about this disease that I am so disappointed about? How do I thank you for this?*

Needless to say, things weren't going well, and the gratitude was not coming easily. I started to cry because I was thinking that it was either I get this figured out and get a thank you to God written or I lose a sister. It was like a bargain, *quid pro quo*. Write it and all is well and you've saved your sisters, or don't and one's a goner. And it'll be my fault because I didn't write the note. But I had no clue how to go about it.

The thought of another one of my sisters going through this was unbearable to me. I went from crying to sobbing, and I couldn't even see my paper anymore through all the tears.

While all this was going on, my pen had just started going. The entire time I felt like it was almost like the pen was moving on its own. I couldn't even see what I was writing. It was the most insane thing I'd ever experienced. The only thing I was thinking while my pen moved wildly across the page was, *What am I writing?*

When I finally put my pen down, I came up with this letter, a thank-you note to God. I read it again, and I was amazed by it. It was as if someone else had taken over, because I just thought, *Why would I write that? That wasn't even in my head.* I did though, and this is what it said:

> Dear God, guardian angels, guides, and all,
>
> I am writing you this letter so you know just how I feel. My spirit is so well connected to you, my heart aches when I stray to the wrong path. I trust you whole-heartedly and welcome you to control the paths in my life. I welcome you all into my life and my home to be a part of my family.
>
> I am so sorry for my wrongdoings—especially in my inability to trust and be thankful through this part of my life—and I ask with a genuine heart for forgiveness. I am so grateful to have all who connect to my spirit for the good of all God's will. I am grateful for all that has been given to us spiritually, financially, physically, mentally, emotionally, and I am grateful for a healthy family.
>
> With all my love and devotion,
> Jeanne.

After the letter was finished, I looked up and asked, "Okay, God, what do you want me to do this thank-you note? What *do* you do with a letter to God? Do I put it in the mail? Do I stamp it? Do I throw it in the air? How do I know if it gets to you?"

"You'll know what to do with it," was all God had to say.

The next night, Duane and I were talking, and I told him about the thank-you note.

"I had to plea bargain to save my sisters," I explained.

"You wrote a thank-you note, didn't you?"

"Yeah," I said, surprised that he knew what I had done. "I'm not gonna let one of my sisters be taken by this."

"You know why you did that, don't you?" Duane asked, staring right at me.

"Well, yeah," I said. "Because God told me to. I'm not going to lose one of my sisters to cancer."

"You know where the letter is gonna go, don't you?" he asked me with this expression that told me even if I didn't know, he did.

"No, I don't know what I'm supposed to do with it," I told him. "You can't mail a letter to God. He told me I would know."

"You're supposed to write a book," Duane said very matter-of-factly.

"Me write a book?" I scoffed. "That's pathetic. I don't have anything that anybody wants to hear."

"Jeanne, people ask you all the time, what are you going through—what *we* are going through. This could answer that," he said, putting his hand out on top of mine. "That needs to go in a book. You're writing a thank you to God, and it'll be a book."

Like everything I've gone through with cancer, I met this with resistance. The entire thing seemed so over-whelming and beyond my reach. I didn't even know the first step to starting such a thing. It was kind of like going through chemo or bumping into a wall. It was an obstacle that seemed bigger than life and intimidating just to think about. To me, it was just more turmoil.

"I don't know if I want to do that," I said.

"You have to," Duane told me, and he was right. I had to. And I did.

# CHAPTER TWO:

# WHERE I CAME FROM

I grew up surrounded by lots of yellow and even more siblings. I was raised with my nine brothers and sisters on the same 160-acre farm that my dad grew up on, and everywhere you looked on the place there was yellow. Our house was two stories and yellow. There was a yellow shop building where everyone knew my dad would be after dark, welding or creating something. He was a genius at crafting things to make our lives easier. Out in the pasture there was a yellow barn that housed forty cows, and there was a yellow milk house separate from the barn. We had a yellow detached two-car garage and a yellow pump house. There was also a chicken coop, woodshed, pig house, and a pole shed where we stacked the bales of hay, and all of it was yellow. You couldn't escape the color once you stepped foot on our family's farm. Our place was so full of yellow that we always got teased about living in a yellow submarine. If I had to describe my childhood as a color, yellow would undoubtedly be the color I would choose.

Yellow wasn't the only thing I remember about my childhood, though. The most important part of all that yellow was the people who lived within it, namely my mom and dad. My dad was a farmer and a Triple-F

Feeds dealer for the neighborhood, and he was a farmer to the core. He was six foot two, balding, 198 pounds, and most importantly, he was 100 percent Polish and proud of it. He loved everything about his heritage, from the music to the cuisine.

*Sylvester Oldakowski aka "Daddy"*

Another thing about my dad was that he had big everything—big nose, big ears, big feet (size twelve)—and a big heart to match. His legs were so long that it took several steps to make up one of his. And those lanky legs of his were always moving, always working, and you hardly ever saw him just sitting still.

Then there was my mom. Just like Daddy, my mom was a worker bee. She spent her days keeping up with all the kids and the nights working as a registered nurse. She did all this while she struggled with her weight; she was an emotional eater. She was five foot six inches and weighed 350 pounds, but she didn't let that slow her down. Mom was also one you'd never lose in a crowd. She always wore bright-pink lipstick and bright-colored blouses (perhaps it was her love for bright things that caused all the yellow around the farm) with polyester pants that were often cut off to be pedal pushers, and these big, round, brown glasses that were perched on her small nose.

*Ann Oldakowski aka "Mommy"*

Where my dad had giant features, my mom was just the opposite. She had tiny little hands and little ears to complement them. Her face was sweet and round, which, coupled with her small features, made her look just as lovable as she was. What I remember most about her, though, was that she was generous. She gave first and took last, and she spoke from her heart. She and my dad were an amazing couple of people to be raised by. Watching them, we learned some of the most important things a person could ever learn from life; we saw hard work, generosity, and also overwhelming humbleness.

Of the two, Dad was the quiet one. He never said a whole lot, but he was always there. Mom was a little more outgoing and extroverted at home. You could hear her singing all around the house, and she was also not shy about her plump body, as she would often dress with the doors wide open. She was certainly the more assertive of the two. Anytime we wanted to go with our friends, Dad would say, "Ask your mother, and if your mother says yes, then I'm okay with that."

Although Dad was reserved, he was stern when he needed to be, but he always had a soft heart. When something went wrong, he was always the one to talk to us girls to make sure that we were okay. And he had this great smile, even with his false teeth.

Dad was quite the jokester, too. There were certain things he'd do pretty regularly just to get a laugh. He had lost all the fingers on his left hand in a farming accident except his pinky, and he used to tease us, "You better not suck on your fingers. I sucked my thumb, and it fell off. And then I sucked my other fingers, and they fell off, too."

He also used to have great fun trying to trick us. He and his brother looked a lot alike—the same balding heads and build. They used to try to make us think that our uncle was Daddy. And when we'd grab his leg and realize we were fooled, they'd laugh and laugh. They got us every time. He also had this thing that he said was a squirrel call. It was a little copper pipe that curled around. He'd put flour in the end of it and then spring it on unsuspecting people—sometimes on our boyfriends when they'd come by. He'd hand it to them to try, and when they blew on the pipe, flour would poof in their faces.

Between the two of them, my mom and dad, with their quirks and their talents, did their best to make sure all the kids grew up the right way and learned the value of hard work, which brings me to the next memory I have of my childhood: chores.

We had plenty of chores to do in all those yellow buildings scattered across our farm. Because my dad farmed for a living and did so without any paid help, he had so much to do that he needed us to help him, a lot. Growing up with so many responsibilities, hard work was something we learned about from an early age. We made our own feed by hand to sell to neighboring farmers. We also had cows, pigs, chickens, ducks, and guinea hens, which were the girls' responsibility to feed twice a day, and then we'd come inside and make sure all the people were fed, too. We pumped water for the cows by hand every morning and every night. Then there was the huge garden we had that the girls tended and harvested from several times a week. I remember the gardening well because Mom would usually come out in her home-dyed bra and cutoff pants to help. We just prayed no company would show up on those days.

We also had to milk cows and take the milk to this massive tank pail by pail. It could be grueling, but it was character building to say the least.

Another particularity about the way I was raised was the kind of medical attention we got growing up. Since Mom was an RN, she always treated us at home. My sister had kidney problems, so she went in to the doctor a lot, but other than that there was one broken arm and probably only three other trips to the doctor between all ten children. Mom treated us with Epsom salt, and that pretty much took care of everything. If one of us had any kind of stomach problems, Mom doled out the Pepto Bismol to the whole lot of us, and the problem was solved. That was about it for medical attention at our house, salt and the pink stuff. We didn't even take vitamins, but we ate plenty of fresh vegetables, we always had square meals, and we drank milk that came straight from the cow. You couldn't get any more organic than us, and we were seldom sick. We had far more injuries than illnesses, and those were carelessness for the most part, the result of stepping on a hayfork or a nail, something like that.

Growing up a farmer's kid, we all also learned how to live pretty simply. We didn't even have an indoor bathroom until 1978. Before that, we had one toilet, and it was an outhouse. I trained myself to ignore my thirst on days that it was below freezing. If you think sitting on a toilet seat in a house during the coldest part of winter is uncomfortable, you should try sitting on one in an outhouse. You could tell when it was bitter cold outside by my family's liquid intake during dinner.

If it hovered around the twenties or lower, not a milk glass was touched during supper.

For quite some time, the simplicity of living we experienced at home also extended to our school. Until I was a second grader, we all went to country school. At the little rural school, everyone was alike. We were all farmers' kids who had to do chores before school and wore tattered clothes. It didn't matter what you looked like or how you were dressed. You could wear the same thing three days in a row and no one even batted an eye. Everything at the school lined up with how we were raised. It made things easy, and it also kept us from thinking that we needed a lot of material things to feel content, which was a good thing because looking back, we didn't have too much that wasn't necessity. We were most definitely not at risk of being materialistic.

Not even Christmas was a time for luxury in our household. More often than not, we'd all just make gifts for one another rather than going into town and buying something off a shelf. Since there were so many kids, we'd draw names and then each of us would give our homemade gift to the person whose name we drew.

As kids, we weren't always completely selfless, though. Even if we were raised by parents who would give anyone anything they needed, we were kids at the end of the day. My sister got two dollars the year she drew my name, and she decided to get me a set of thirty-nine cent pick-up sticks and used the rest of the money on herself. I was more amused than anything when I realized what she'd done, and so was everyone else. We decided to make pick-up sticks a Christmas tradition after that. Ever since then, we give pick-up sticks to each other back and forth. Sometimes they're nothing but snipped off pieces from wire hangers stuck in a jar, but there's always some kind of pick-up sticks.

Needless to say, in almost every way our farm was sparse where luxuries were concerned, but we did always have a car to get around in; these big ugly cars, always bright colors like pink or yellow. We generally didn't go out much, but when we did, it was quite a spectacle. Mom and Dad would sit in the front with one of my sisters between them. The rest of us would stack up in the back, biggest on the bottom. The littlest ones got the back window. I always thought it was embarrassing to be hanging out in the back window and see my friends.

Dad was a heavy smoker, so along with ten kids and two adults, there was also always a heavy nicotine cloud that traveled with us in our car. When we would get to church or wherever it was we were going, the yellow smoke would come rolling out with all us kids. With all those kids and all that smoke traveling in one car, it was probably a good thing we didn't go out too much.

Although the number of kids and our limited funds kept us from traveling too much, it didn't keep Mom and Dad from having at least a little bit of a social life. Once a month they'd have something they called Mothers' Club. The mothers would get together at one of their houses—on my parents' turn they'd play cards, eat, and talk. Mom would set up a large twelve-foot-long folding table my dad had made in the middle of the living room for the women, and the guys would sit in the kitchen around our big homemade table and play dice or cards.

During these gatherings, all the children would be upstairs. Because our house was a hundred years old and had never been updated, there was no heater upstairs so we we'd open a little flap in the wall and the heat from the wood stove would vent up to our rooms and heat the upstairs so all the kids didn't freeze. Generally we were only up there to sleep, but on the days all the adults would come over, we needed to stay upstairs and out of the way.

We did what we were told and stayed upstairs, but we still found a way to peek in on what was going on under our feet. While everyone was downstairs having a great time, we'd try to peep through the little flap we used to let heat in to see what was going on and to scope out the food spread that Mom had put out so we could decide what we would get once everyone was gone. The moment we would hear all the cranking, popping, and whirling of the neighbor's car engine in the drive, we'd all race downstairs to claim our own share of the feast Mom had made.

Mothers' Club wasn't the only time Mom fed more than just the family. Whenever people would stop at the farm because they'd gotten lost or broken down or were just there to visit, you could bet they weren't going to leave for at least three or four hours. Dad would go out and repair things, give directions, or bend their ear. When he could, he'd lure them from the driveway to the house, and then they couldn't leave until they ate. Mom was there and ready to cook anytime she heard a car pulling into the drive. It was never anything fancy, but it was always delicious. Our meals were always simple, something that Mom could get cheap and stretch a long way, but they were good, hearty meals, and they were there for whomever stopped by. If someone ever left our house hungry, it was his or her own fault. Nobody ever felt out of place in our house either. My parents were experts in hospitality.

---

With ten kids to feed and clothe, my parents needed us to do more than just feed the animals and cook meals whenever we could. I decided at twelve that I was ready for my first job, and so I started babysitting for a family with seven kids. Their parents worked in bars. They lived in a tiny trailer house, and I would watch all seven of the kids, and, because my mom had taught me it was the right thing to do, I would also cook their meals and be sure that when I left the place, it was cleaner than when I got there. I got paid fifty cents an hour to do that, if I got paid at all. I would be there taking care of all the kids until after midnight since the parents' jobs were in bars, and sometimes the parents didn't come home at all, which put me in a tough spot for a variety of reasons, mostly that I had chores to do and school the next day. The work wasn't worth the pay, that is for sure, but I did it for two years because work was work.

When I was fourteen, my mom got a call from a lady she knew who worked at a convent and was hiring.

"I know you are farmers and you have a lot of daughters," she said to my mom. "I've worked with two of your daughters, and they are wonderful, so I was wondering if I could have another one."

"Well, I have one, but she's only fourteen," my mom explained to the woman.

"I'll take her," the woman replied without a second thought.

So the next day I went to work for a convent for retired nuns, and I worked there for seven years as the nurse's aid. We helped get the sisters up, dressed them, got them ready for their daily activities, and then put them to bed later. Everything you would do in a nursing home to care for someone, we did for them.

Once I started working as a nurse's aid, I hardly had a moment to myself. I would be up before daybreak to do my chores, go to school, work afterward until about eleven thirty at night, come home to do my homework, and then start the next day again at 5:00 a.m. Before we went to school, we had to have all our chores done and breakfast on the table. Dad was a hard-working farmer, and everything had to be a well-oiled machine, so it was important that none of us missed a beat.

Growing up the way I did was tiring, and it could feel like torture every now and then, but it also felt really good to know I was constantly doing something that mattered and that I was doing it for my family. It was arduous, but it was rewarding because I was giving back to two people who truly deserved it. I had them to thank for everything, really. For the food I ate, the roof over my head, but most importantly, I appreciated what kind of person they taught me to be. I thought I'd learned about all I needed to know by the time I was ready to graduate from school. I did learn a lot, but I had no idea how many lessons on life were still awaiting me, and it was going to take heartbreak and also a lot of soul-searching to teach me. That's really where my story starts, with the lessons I learned from something that is so ugly but in the end can really be a teacher. So the rest of this book contains the lessons that I have learned from cancer. I hope that maybe they are able to help others skip the hardest parts of the battle and see sooner what took me a while to see myself.

# LESSON 1:

# VULNERABILITY IS NOT A WEAKNESS

In December 2005, Mom broke her femur, which left her with a left, above-the-knee amputation that she despised. She wound up with an infection in her stump, but she didn't say anything about it because she didn't want to be a burden on the family.

One day when I was at the nursing home visiting, I came in and asked if I could see how she was healing. I pulled back the sheet, and what I saw made the blood drain from my face. Her leg was severely infected to the point it was oozing.

"Mommy, how long has that been oozing green?" I asked, trying not to sound as shocked as I was.

"Jeanne, just shut up," she snapped, pulling the sheet back over the infected stump. "The nurses know about it."

At that point in my life, I had to become an RN. I knew that my mom's infection was not a good sign. She insisted that she was fine, though, and that there was nothing to worry about. That was her motto when it came to her own health: everything is fine and no one should worry themselves. Unfortunately, she was wrong. That night the surgeon was notified, and Mom ended up in intensive care. She died less than twelve hours after I had asked her about the infection, which caused severe sepsis. It was the first time I felt real heartbreak, and it completely tore my world apart.

When she was alive, Mom lived by the simple rule that you always go to work or school unless you are dead or dying. You didn't go to the doctor for every sniffle, and you didn't lie around in bed just because you didn't feel well, or at least *she* didn't. She was always concerned with the well-being of others and made sure everyone else was okay, but she put herself last. As long as everyone else was doing fine, that's all that mattered to her. It was devastatingly noble, and it cost her life in the end. I never really thought about the consequences of never thinking of yourself. It seemed the most honorable trait one could possess, but after my mom's death, I had to reevaluate some things.

My mom's reluctance to see a doctor for anything that didn't have her on her deathbed and her refusal to let anyone make a fuss over her was a trait that she passed down to me. Until I hit my forties, I seldom went to the doctor unless it stopped me from going to work. I treated everything homeopathically, and I did my best to keep it to myself. I still feel like a complainer when I go to the doctor, but once I became a mother, I never thought twice whether or not to take my children to the doctor if they were ill; we went without hesitation. I could never bring myself to do the same, though. It was a learned habit that I couldn't shake.

With my mom's passing, I began to realize that there were some things I was going to struggle with that I had never thought of, some learned behaviors I hadn't realized would be problematic. I had trouble responding to my body in a way I needed to, and I would have to learn to do that.

As we laid my mom in her final resting place, things became a little clearer to me, and I was beginning to see that it was okay to put yourself first sometimes, that it was not a sin to be vulnerable and admit that you needed some looking after yourself. Had Mom had the opportunity to learn the same lesson, she might still be with us today.

———————

Mom wasn't the only one who wasn't crazy about slowing down and taking time to take care of herself. My dad was also someone who rarely stepped foot in a doctor's office when he was feeling bad. And as ironic as it is since I have problems taking myself to the doctor, I was the one nominated by my siblings to be the medical tattle tale in the family, so it was always my job to get Dad there, even though several of my other siblings actually worked in the medical field as well.

Whenever Dad was sick, I'd say, "Hey, Daddy, let's go fishing." He'd shave and get ready to go fishing, and I'd take a detour to the medial clinic. I resented the role at times because I felt it robbed us of having a normal father-daughter connection, but I was glad that someone was making sure that he was being taken care of. For the longest time, I did this without realizing that while I was battling Dad to get him to the doctor and always explaining to him how it was okay to take care of yourself, I was ignoring my own advice.

Sometimes when I could tell how upset he was with me for dragging him to the clinic, I wanted to grab him and say, "Look, Daddy, we're all human. We all get sick, and we all need help sometimes, everyone in the world, so you don't need to pretend you're not like everyone else. It's okay."

I needed to give myself that speech, though. I needed to realize that I was also human like everyone else, and part of being a human was being vulnerable at times. I had Daddy to take care of though, and my own kids, so it was easy for me to ignore my own lessons. I had others to take care of.

In June of 2008, Dad fell in the garage, and afterward he noticed blood in his urine. Luckily he let us know, so we took him in for an MRI to see what was going on. I didn't need to be an RN to know that blood showing up where it shouldn't was cause for concern. I instinctively knew that something was going on. I didn't need a medical book or a doctor to tell me.

Dad had his MRI done, and I tried to prepare myself for whatever news the doctor had for us, so when the doctor said that everything looked fine and he didn't see anything out of the ordinary, I was a little baffled. I did feel a quick sense of relief, but that was gone before the doctor even left the room. All my worries should have dissipated once the doctor told us all was well, but for me it was hanging around and gnawing at me. I knew that things weren't fine.

The weeks following, Daddy just wasn't the same. He never seemed to feel himself. He was weak and pale, and he never had much of an appetite. His complexion had been gray and waxy since Mom had passed, though, so I tried to convince myself that he was just lonely and that was the root of all the problems. Even though I was constantly telling myself that the doctors said things were fine and that what Dad was experiencing was probably just the physical effects of mourning his wife of so many decades, I never really believed it. Because his health was basically my responsibility, which I was happy to have, I kept a close eye on him, and I didn't like what I was seeing.

When July rolled around and blood in his urine persisted, I took Dad back to the doctor a few times, and my sister took him once. The last time he went, he was bleeding quite a bit. He seemed to be losing color by the day, and I was having trouble believing that it was just loneliness causing him to look more dead than alive. On the last time, since there was so much blood loss, we took him to a little town hospital hoping they may have something more substantial to tell us than "everything looks fine" when it so clearly wasn't.

"There's blood in his urine," the doctor told us. That was it. We didn't need someone to tell us that there was blood; we needed someone to tell us why, but searching for an answer to my dad's health issues seemed to be as impossible as searching for the Holy Grail.

With the diagnosis of "he has blood in his urine," we decided to take him to a bigger hospital. This time we were resolved not to leave until we had a better answer, or at least a more conclusive one since the answer we got was anything but "better."

They did biopsies, and on the Fourth of July, the doctors called to tell us what had been causing the problems.

"We have the results back," the doctor began in a tone that was so remorseful he might as well have been giving Dad's eulogy over the phone that day. "He has masses on his stomach, prostate, and bladder. It's cancer."

"So what do we do now?" I asked as I felt my guts jump up and wrap around my heart.

"It's fairly aggressive cancer, and since he is eighty-three, the treatment would likely be harder on him than the cancer."

*Kitana 3 years old & "Papa Syl"*

So that was it. They didn't even give him the option. They said he would have three to six months left. But Dad said he'd just have to make the best of it, and that is what we did. He'd actually gone out and bought a four-wheeler just a week before, so he'd already started. I knew in the depths of my being that something was wrong, so I'd convinced Dad to go out and buy something for himself. He'd spent his life never spending a cent on anything that he wanted, only things he needed, so I told him it was time to change that. He decided to do it, and once we brought the four-wheeler home, he said, "You know, if I thought I was going to die, I wouldn't have bought this." I told him to keep that attitude, because once your attitude slips, so does everything else.

Even though the doctor had given him a timetable, I wanted him to enjoy every moment he had. He'd spent so long working nonstop to keep the farm going and to make sure we were all taken care of that a lot had slipped past him. It seems to be a common trend with people today. People don't realize all they're missing until they're told they have a short time. I'm sure there have been many people who never started truly living until their lives were threatened. It's easy to take things for granted when we assume that things will always be just as they are. They won't though. The one constant in life is change, and sometimes change means losing someone who you always thought would be there. After losing Mom and then Dad's diagnosis, I certainly began to take the time to really soak up those I love and every little beautiful part of life.

It took Dad a little time to digest what he was told, but I hoped that, if nothing else, he would spend his last months living like he never had and appreciating the things that we often feel are insignificant.

It took a few weeks for Dad to pick himself back up. For a little while he was really depressed, but we kept him busy and told the neighbors to check in on him regularly. He had a lot of company around to keep his spirits up. With ten kids, there was never really any rest anyway. But he said he needed some time to himself because he was tired. So we put a sign on his door when he needed rest—of course he never locked the door.

Dad struggled quite a bit with learning how to be something he never had been: vulnerable. He had a lot of problems with his catheter getting plugged up with blood clots, and he'd need help getting it flushed out. He'd call me for help, and he'd cry, "Jeanne, I'm so sorry that you have to see me like this."

"Dad, you know that I would do anything for you," I'd reassure him. "I just want you to ask because I don't know if I'm doing the right thing."

My niece moved in to help him out. She had grown up with my parents, so she was really like Grandpa's little girl. When she started having to help with his catheter, he was mortified. Once she heard him crying out from upstairs. She wasn't sure what to do, so she called me.

"Should I go help Grandpa?" she asked me, panicked. Nobody wanted to see him at his worst, and he didn't want anyone to see him either, so it was a difficult situation for everyone.

I coached my niece over the phone on how to help unplug the catheter, and they both cried. The entire thing was so hard-hitting, and he was so exhausted most of the time. He felt like such a burden. He had spent his whole life raising his ten children so that they could take care of themselves and never feel burdened by any sort of hardship, and now he felt that he was that hardship he'd tried so hard to help us avoid.

My dad's feelings about letting us help were the hardest thing for me to deal with after the cancer diagnosis. It made me so sad. I didn't understand then because I always felt like if you spent your life taking care of ten children that it should be expected when you age that they look after you. I couldn't comprehend why he had to put up such a fight when all we wanted to do was help him.

I didn't really understand at that time though, but soon enough I would. I didn't know what it felt like to be a parent suddenly relying on a child or to be a strong person suddenly drained of strength. The fact is, it's hard to be vulnerable and to let someone else take care of you, especially when you've spent your life as the foundation that everyone stood on. He was always the responsible one, the head of the house—the dad. His role was to be in charge of things, to tell us what to do, and suddenly that was ripped from him. The thing was, though, all his kids wanted from him once he was sick was to let them help.

As I witnessed my dad sob and apologize through every catheter placement, the lesson I had learned from my mom's passing came back to me, and this time it was even clearer than before. Watching Dad, I saw how difficult it could be to surrender pride and to be absolutely vulnerable, but I also learned something from my side: there was no need to feel like vulnerability was a weakness, per se, but rather a time to allow those who love you do what they could to help you. As hard as it could be, vulnerability could even be a tool to bring a family closer together. Dad's dependence on us didn't make us resent him or think less of him. It made us come together to do something that was all of our priority, to help him when he needed it.

So we all did our best to take care of him and be sure that he didn't feel like a burden. As we took turns checking in on Dad, cleaning up around the house, and making sure that he got everything he needed, I thought of another valuable lesson in all the chaos: being good to your family pays off in the end. Because my dad put us first, we did the same for him. Mom always used to say that what goes around comes around. If you were a nasty, selfish person, that was all you'd get in return. My family was generous, for the most part, and we learned it from our parents. Because they'd been selfless with us, it was what we instinctively fell to when we saw that they needed help.

The experiences I had losing my mom and dad were heart-wrenching, but they were preparing me for my own battle to come. God gave me the opportunity to stand on one side of illness, being the healthy caretaker. I don't believe that my parents passing was only for me and my family to learn something we needed to learn, but I do believe that God was doing his best to show me something I'd been missing, several things actually. I was learning that life is precious and we need to cherish the tiniest things about it, and most of all, that when we are at our weakest, that is when we should let family come in to help us—that is what family is for.

# LESSON 2:

# LEARN TO LISTEN TO YOUR BODY, YOUR SPIRIT, AND EVERYTHING AROUND YOU

*Listen to your inner voice if you don't get the answers that you are comfortable with, keep looking. Do not avoid the voice from within.*

Just after my dad was diagnosed with cancer, so was my sister, Beth. She was a pretty proactive person about her health, so she actually found the lump herself during a self-examination. It was in her left breast. She found the lump in May and decided she'd wait until June to act on it to make sure it wasn't just something that her hormones had caused. It was still there in June, so she acted upon it and had a mammogram, which came back positive. After that, she had biopsies, and they found two lumps that were cancer in the middle of June.

Beth didn't tell us about the cancer immediately because it was just after Dad had been diagnosed. She waited a little while to make the announcement to give us time to recover from our first shock. One evening when five of us were out camping, she stopped by the campsite.

"Since a lot of you are here, I've got something to tell you," she said, standing in the middle of the group. "I have cancer."

My knee-jerk reaction was to think that this was a dirty prank of hers. I couldn't believe she had the gall to say such a thing right after Dad was having so many health problems, but I found out that it was no prank at all. The same summer my dad was given three to six months to live, my sister was diagnosed with breast cancer. I'd never heard of anyone who'd experienced such a thing. It felt a little unreal.

At the end of June, Beth had a lumpectomy, and they found cancer in her lymph nodes. We had always been attached at the hip before the diagnosis, and I wanted to be supportive through the process, but I could feel something change after she told us she had cancer. I was there, along with almost all my other siblings, the day of her surgery, and I would take her to doctor's visits, but even though I was there, it felt like I wasn't, like I was in Texas and she was in Minnesota. It was suddenly like my sister and I had a long-distance relationship.

It was strange how cancer changed things for us. We used to be open with one another, and she was one of my closest friends, but then cancer came along, and I felt tongue-tied around my own sister. I was afraid

I'd say the wrong thing and make everything worse for her. I wanted to help and comfort her, but I didn't know how, and the last thing I wanted to do was trip over my own words and make matters worse. With my dad, there was no treatment or talk or survival, so this was foreign territory for me, and I wasn't sure how to approach it.

Along with being terrified that I would say the wrong thing, I was also afraid of losing her. I avoided spending time at her house, and with just Beth in general, because I was convinced that one day I'd show up and she'd have just vanished, disappeared from our lives forever and ever. I didn't want to get attached because I didn't know when she'd no longer be there. I just kept my distance in an effort to safeguard myself. Now I realize that it was not the way to handle it. In fact, if I could do it all over again, I would've done the opposite, but at the time there was something that paralyzed me, and I just couldn't be there for her. And it wasn't just me, either. All my sisters had the same response. We were all too afraid of causing more pain or letting ourselves get hurt to maintain our relationship with our sister when she needed us to.

Even though all my sisters and I started to dodge Beth after her diagnosis, she was sure to contact us often to remind us that it was important to get ourselves checked. She turned into a real breast cancer awareness advocate, and she was on all of us to get regular mammograms and to be proactive in protecting ourselves. Every time she'd call, it'd be the same conversation.

"Hey, Jeanne, I was just calling to see if you've gone in for a mammogram yet," she'd say, probably already knowing what I was about to say.

"Not yet," I would tell her. "I've just been too busy."

"It's important, Jeanne," she'd scold. "More important than whatever you were busy with. The key to prevention is getting checked."

I'd always tell her that I would be sure to make an appointment soon, but I pushed it out of my mind as soon as we were off the phone, or try to anyway. I've always been small busted, so I brushed it off as, "Nah, with breasts this size, there's nothing to worry about." I'd spent my life being teased for my small chest, so I wasn't about to entertain the idea that there was something harmful growing inside it. I was doing my best to ignore the reality of the situation by turning a deaf ear to my sister, which wasn't doing me any favors.

It wasn't just my sister that had been trying to get my attention. I think people have become masters at ignoring cues and signs, especially that come from nature, and I realized after I was diagnosed a subtle hint that I had missed for years. As strange as it may sound, our family dog, a Shih tzu named Cheech, was trying to tell me long before the doctors that something was going on.

For two years prior to my diagnosis, every time I would sit on the couch, Cheech would jump up and nudge me in the breast, in the very same spot they found the cancer. It wasn't just a couple of times, either. He would do this repeatedly, and it went on for months. I'd be sitting there, watching the news, and Cheech would hop up in my lap and tap his nose to my chest over and over and then just jump down, only to return again three or four more times to do the same thing.

Cheech's behavior certainly caught my attention, but I didn't give him enough credit or give it the attention that it deserved. Sure, I found it strange that all of the sudden our family dog, who had never been allowed on the couch, was ignoring the house rules and was so drawn to my chest, but I never considered that he knew something that I did not. I probably didn't want to think of Cheech's gesture as an indicator that something was wrong either because oftentimes paying attention to the small things can be intimidating. I've learned though that being in touch with the small things should be seen as an opportunity, not a curse, to take action and have at least a bit more control of your own fate.

Although it did take me a bit to accept that it was time to get checked, I did finally throw in the towel and got checked. It was actually a chiropractor's visit that led me to my first mammogram. I went in to have my back adjusted, but when I saw the X-rays of my spine and neck, I realized that I had more problems than a few out of place vertebrae.

After the chiropractor took the X-rays, he came in and put them up for me to see. I immediately noticed a spot that had nothing to do with my neck or back. I could tell by the chiropractor's words that he had noticed it, too. As we both sat and stared at the X-ray, the doctor finally got to it.

"Is there anything on your X-ray you'd like to go over?" he asked me. "It doesn't have to be about your back. Just let me know."

I knew what he was getting at, but I didn't say a word. I just sat silent with my eyes fixed on the spot in my left breast. It seemed to grow in size as I stared. It was like I could feel it in me. My mouth went dry, and I could feel the blood rushing to my brain as I tried to wrap my head around the glaring spot in the X-ray. *Oh my God, it's happening to me*, I thought as the doctor began to talk again, since it was clear I had no intention of saying anything.

I didn't hear a word the chiropractor said after that. I could feel words hit the back of my throat, but I couldn't force them out. I did want to talk to him about the spot, but at the same time I had no idea how I could possibly talk to a chiropractor about a spot in my breast. What could a chiropractor *do* about it anyway?

I decided not to say anything to the man I went to when I had a crick in my neck, but I did go home and make an appointment with my general doctor. I was all nerves the entire time. This thing I'd been avoiding for so long was finally forcing me to deal with it, and it had tossed me so far out of my comfort zone that I didn't know if I'd ever get back to it.

I went in, and my doctor scheduled a mammogram. When I went in for the mammogram, one mammogram turned into twenty, and then twenty turned into twenty-five. The twenty-fifth time I was having my breast smashed, the technician said, "Oh, we're just not used to this machine," as she gave it another go.

"Just give us some time and things will be okay," she assured me.

I tried to stay positive, but it was the most nerve-wracking experience I'd ever had, and I was less than comfortable wearing only a hospital gown as thick as tissue paper (and as comfortable) in the Arctic-like rooms they had me in. When the mammogram finally took, they did indeed find something.

"There is a spot the doctor is concerned with," the nurse explained.

I had prepared myself for this, but no amount of preparation really does the trick in these kinds of situations. I nodded my head and tried to keep calm as I listened to her explain what we'd do next.

"We're going to set up biopsies and an ultrasound for today, so you can follow me to the waiting area, and we'll let you know when the doctor is ready."

With that, the nurse took me to a waiting room, and from the waiting room they set up biopsies and an ultrasound for me. Once they were ready, I was led across the hallway, clothes in hand and still wearing the tissue paper gown, and had an ultrasound done.

As the ultrasound technician prepped for the ultrasound, I was baffled when he squirted the ultrasound gel on my right breast.

"It was my left breast actually that I found something in," I told him, trying not to sound condescending but making sure he knew that he was doing the wrong breast.

He looked up and gave a faint smile and assured me, "No, I have the paperwork right here, and it says that we're to check the right side."

"Can you check your paperwork again?" I asked, a little more persistent than I had been the first time. "I think that you're mistaken, and I'll just have to do this again if we do the right side."

The technician checked the paperwork again and confirmed that it was the right side he was to check, and they ended up finding three spots that were suspicious, so they set me up with surgery. Because I was so small, they initially decided to do the biopsy right there in the clinic but then decided not to because there was a risk of puncturing the lung, so they ended up deciding to set me up with a surgeon. That meant I would go to the medical plaza and have a full surgery under general anesthesia to biopsy my right side. I nodded my head while the doctor went through the process. My body went through waves of tension and numbness as I took it all in. I felt like I was watching someone else get the news the whole time.

The doctor set up the surgery, and we decided not to tell anyone in the family yet. I opted to keep it secret mostly for Beth. I figured she was already dealing with my dad and with herself, so she didn't need something else on her plate. I felt that I would tell them when the time was right, but now was not the time. I also wasn't ready to tell my two children, Kira, who had just gotten engaged, and my son Brad, so my husband, Duane, and I would handle this just the two of us for the time being.

August came in a hurry, and it was time to do the surgery. The night before the surgery was a fitful one for me, and probably for Duane as well. I tried my best to sleep, but I had trouble powering my brain down long enough to drift off. Finally the morning came, and we got up from our sleepless night and prepared to go to the plaza.

I had surgery at 9:00 a.m., so we got there at around half past seven. When the room was ready for me, I went in and slipped into my little bear hugger gown. These gowns are heated, so at least I wouldn't be in tissue paper this time. They sent Duane out to the waiting room until I was dressed and ready to go, and then they were going to let him come back in to see me before the surgery. As I was dressing, though, a nurse popped in.

"Jeanne, let's go do one last mammogram," she said as she tugged on the stethoscope that hung from her neck.

"Really?" I said, a little confused since this wasn't the game plan. "I had twenty-five yesterday. What is one more today gonna show that twenty-five yesterday didn't?"

"I know it's frustrating," she empathized. "Let's just do it to be sure."

"Okay," I replied with a shrug, and we trekked through the entire plaza to get to the mammogram station again. Just as before, one mammogram turned into several, and I sat, freezing in a gown and slippers, to wait for the outcome. *Why are we doing this?* I thought as I tapped a nervous foot on the cold tile beneath my feet.

As I waited for the nurse to return, my mind went wild. I thought, *Maybe things can change and they aren't coming back. Maybe the spots just disappeared and no one will need to do anything today.* After what seemed like twelve or more hours (it was actually no more than half an hour though) of rigorous toe tapping and thoughts run amuck, still nobody had come to tell me anything.

Finally just when I was convinced I'd never see anything again but that cold, sterile room, the nurse reappeared, and she said, "Sorry it took so long. We've got the doctor looking at your X-rays, and we'll get back to you as soon as we can. I promise we won't forget about you." She smiled, turned, and left me there all alone in the X-ray room once again.

When you have to have biopsies done, waiting is the worst thing someone can make you do, and I was doing a lot of it at that point. As I sat in an uncomfortable chair that had freezing cold vinyl wrapped round its worn padding, I tried to think about anything *but* why I was there. I started to think that hell must be something like a waiting room in an oncology center.

There weren't enough distractions in the world that day to keep me from fixating on why in the world I was stuck in the X-ray room. I knew the doctors were looking at my X-rays, and I couldn't help but think of all the possible reasons they were taking so long to come back to get me and let me go on to my biopsy. I ran the gamut of emotional responses to the situation, too. I got angry about the whole thing; then I began to plead with God, *Please, God, you have the wrong girl,* I explained with my hands clasped tightly together in my lap. *Those X-rays yesterday were not mine.* I was just crying and pleading to God, *You have the wrong girl. This is a mistake, and you need to re-divert whatever you find. Not me, it's not supposed to be me. It's supposed to be somebody else.*

As I was explaining to God how he'd made a mix-up, the nurse came in wearing an expression that didn't set my mind at ease.

"Jeanne," she said, "the doctor wants to see you."

*Uh-oh,* I thought. *Now what?* I felt like I was walking the plank that whole morning and I was about to hit the end and crash down into a bottomless ocean full of creatures I wasn't ready to take on.

I got up from my chair, and I left the room I felt I'd been in for ages to go face the doctor yet again. I walked into the doctor's office, and he had his back to me as he sat in a chair and faced a lit screen. He was staring at two X-rays in front of him. I don't know how, but I could tell he was really studying them just by looking at the back of his head. I wondered as I approached him whose X-rays those were he was staring at so intently.

"Jeanne," he finally said as he swung his chair around to face me. "I really don't know what's going on."

"What do you mean you don't know what's going on?" I asked. That isn't something you want a doctor to say to you, ever.

He turned around to the X-ray and said, "I'm looking at your X-ray from yesterday, and we saw three spots, and I don't see any on today's X-rays."

"Whoa," I replied, more confused than ever. "Maybe that's the wrong X-ray." I searched the X-ray for my name and saw on each of them that they were in fact mine. Then I said, "Maybe you took it on the wrong breast."

"No," the doctor replied, "they're from the right breasts."

My confusion abruptly turned to elation. I wanted to burst into to tears of relief. It was like I'd been given a pardon. I immediately thought that God must've heard me; he must've realized that I was the wrong girl. I felt like I'd been reborn in that doctor's office, but at the same time something felt a little off. So twenty-five minutes before my biopsy, the doctor called and canceled the surgery.

"Oh my gosh, really?" I blurted.

"Yep," he verified. "We're gonna cancel surgery." So he called the surgeon, who was already prepped with his team in the surgery room, and they cancelled surgery.

As I made my way back to the room I had been in earlier, I barreled through every emotion on the planet. I was overjoyed that my prayers had worked, but then I got angry because I thought about how this could all come back the next year. My anger then turned to worry, worry about if I'd have to go through the entire thing again since I didn't address it this time, and then there was fear. It was an emotional roller coaster—happy, sad, fear, anger, frustration, and everything in between and on the outskirts.

I finally made it to my room, and I was emotionally spent from the walk. Once I made it back, it seemed like all the nurses avoided me. One came in, and she that I could get dressed and that she was going to remove the IV.

"I can't believe you're pulling out my IV," I said to her as she reached down to get to my hand the IV was in. "We're not done here yet."

The nurse didn't even miss a beat, though. She pulled out the IV and hurried out. As she was leaving, she said again, "You can go ahead and get dressed."

I was fuming about the way she just took the IV out and left because I knew that something was left undone. Everyone else seemed to think differently though. The doctor cancelled the surgery, so there was nothing else to do.

The nurse went to get Duane and brought him back to my room where I sat completely at a loss. I was still in my underwear when the two came into the room.

"What's going on?" he asked, his forehead wrinkled with concern. He thought I was in surgery already, so this was throwing him for a loop.

"They cancelled surgery," I told him with tears rolling down my face. "This time."

"What? They did not."

"They did," I told him again. "They cancelled surgery." Then I told him about the gal that took me to go get another mammogram. "The doctor didn't see anything on the second mammogram."

"Oh my God," he said with a blank expression. "All those mammograms yesterday, and today they didn't see it?"

"Yeah. I don't understand it either."

Duane went through the same emotional trip I had when I heard the news. As he sat in front of me, I could tell which one was coming next. I knew right away how they all went because I'd just gone through them myself. It was like clockwork. I called each one. I thought, *Okay, he's going to be relieved, and next he's going to be angry.* Sure enough, anger showed up right after the joy. I told him to try to calm down when he was angry; then the sadness came, and he started to cry.

"Oh my God," he said through his tears. "We're gonna have to deal with this next year." Right on time. Just like me, he felt broken-hearted by the end.

After we worked our way through the initial shock, we went home, but we still didn't tell Kira or Brad. Although we both should've felt an immense amount of relief that day, neither of us did. Sure, our first response was joy, but it didn't take long for me or my husband to realize that something was amiss. We both wanted to believe that the doctor had just made a mistake the day before and everything was fine, but we instinctively knew that wasn't the case and we should've kept pushing and insisted to go on with the biopsy and look at the left breast as well. They may have had charts and records, but I had instincts, and they were telling me differently.

In the beginning stages of my own journey with cancer, I didn't realize yet the importance of really listening—listening to others, listening to nature, and, most importantly, listening to myself. I had clues all around me to tell me that something was not right, but

I didn't know yet how to put my fear aside and truly hear what was being said to me.

It seems difficult for many of us to slow down and pay attention to the things around us and even ourselves, but it's a vital skill to hone. It's a skill that can alter our lives. When I finally realized what was going on with me, Beth told me, "If you don't like what you find, don't let that fear paralyze you and keep you from acting upon it." She was absolutely right, and I now cherish those words of wisdom, and I hope that those who read this will too.

# LESSON 3:

# IT'S ALL RIGHT TO BE ANGRY

*Anger is a part of the healing process. It is okay to be upset and frustrated with a new diagnosis that intruded into your life.*

Oftentimes when we think about dealing with something like cancer, we immediately think of the importance of positivity, and a positive attitude is vital, but anger also plays a significant role in the process, and no one should feel that it has to be locked away in a little box never to be experienced once a biopsy comes back positive. In fact, anger is necessary, and it helps heal. We don't want to get caught up in it and let it consume us, but if we approach it in the right way, anger can be used to help us get to the next level, and I learned that when dealing with both Beth and my own diagnosis.

When Dad was diagnosed with cancer, it was devastating and it shook us all, but it seemed that Beth's diagnosis hit much harder, probably because it seemed to pour salt in our wounds and it felt like God was, for whatever reason, picking on our family.

I mentioned in the previous chapter that when Beth announced to us she had cancer, I first thought she was playing the most inappropriate prank of all time. When I realized she hadn't stooped so low as to make cancer jokes, I got a little antsy about it, and then suddenly I was just angry. The news came just after Dad had gotten sick, so it felt like our family was caught in a hailstorm and God wasn't providing any shelter for us. The more I thought about it, the more infuriated I was, too. How could God take two people in our family at the same time? *Why* would he do that to us? We were good people who'd worked hard and helped others at every turn. Why were we being punished?

The anger faded eventually, but it had a way of resurfacing from time to time, and for a while I didn't know how to handle it, or if I was wrong to be so mad—if my anger was a weakness or if feeling it meant that I was giving into negativity.

Then came my own diagnosis, which obviously is an entirely different experience because suddenly my own immediate family was directly affected; my husband, children, and grandchildren would now have to go through all this with me, and no one wants to put his or her family through something like that.

When you are the one with cancer, you are terrified when you get the call from the doctor, not just because you're sick but because of what the illness will do to those you love. I believe that much of the anger that both cancer patients and their families feel is born of fear, and they must work through it to get past that fear. For me, the experience with this kind of anger born of fear started at the chiropractor, but it all really came to life a year later.

In September 2009, I was more aware of doing breast exams, but I didn't really know what I was feeling for. Because Beth was never shy about her diagnosis, she let me feel her lump before she had it removed; it was kind of like a hard pea. So I was doing my breast exams monthly, feeling for a little pea, and I also had a scheduled mammogram since the doctor put me on a six-month schedule after my initial scare.

On September 24, I went into a mammogram, and they found two spots on my left side. It didn't even scare me. I wasn't fearful or angry. I just thought, *Oh yeah, those weren't there last year*, or, *Those were there last year and they weren't concerned about them*.

Since I'd gone through it once before, I just thought it was no big deal and things would play out like they had before, so I'd just go home and wait for my call. I knew that they'd call me and say it was all clear or send a letter I always got after exams. I'd be cleared by a letter and go on my merry way. And at first that was how it went. I did get a letter of clearing and a call, but then a week later I got a call back.

"Jeanne, we found two spots on the left," the nurse explained. "We need you to come in and have a biopsy."

I thought, *Oh God, here's my name coming up again.* And honestly, I just kind of figured that they might cancel my biopsies like they had before.

When the doctor first found the spot, he did one more mammogram, and he came into the room, his eyes fixed on the floor, and he kneeled down on the floor beside me.

"Jeanne," he said as he looked up at me and grabbed my hand. "I've got some bad news for you." And then there was silence.

I swallowed the lump in my throat, and I said, "Okay give it to me."

"We've found two spots in your left breast," he said. "We need to do a biopsy."

"Okay, let's do it," I said boldly.

"You're not angry?" he asked, a little shocked by my reaction.

"No," I told him. "Let's just do it."

"I've never had any biopsy person act like this before," he told me.

"Well, let me be the first," I said. "Go ahead and set up an appointment."

"You want to set one up?" he asked.

"Well, whatever works for you," I said. "Just schedule it in."

So my biopsies were scheduled for a week and a half later, and this time no one cancelled them. I showed up, had them done, then went home that day and waited for the news. Still, I tried to convince myself there was nothing to worry about, but this time I wouldn't be sent home with a clear bill of health.

Kira was down in the basement with Duane when the doctor's office called the next week. I picked up the phone, and what I heard changed my life and my family's life forever.

"Jeanne, we found your biopsies were positive," the nurse said.

I'd never felt so many emotions hit at once. I thought the day I was sent home from the plaza without going through with my surgery was the most intense anyone could feel, but I found out that day I heard "biopsies" and "positive" in the same sentence that I was wrong. I wanted to collapse on the floor and scream. I wanted to run downstairs and grab Duane so he could make me feel better. I wanted to keep quiet so no one would know. I wanted to throw up. But most of all, I wanted someone to blame. Could this really happen again?

I tried to keep up with the onslaught of feelings and thoughts that were pounding down all at once, and as I was doing this I was writing everything I could down and I was crying.

"Positive?" I asked, hoping that somehow my questioning it would undo the results.

"Yes," the nurse verified. And down came my world.

In the meantime, Kira had come up from the basement to get something to drink, and as she passed me, she heard the word *positive*. She stopped the second she heard it and snatched the notebook I'd been trying to write the information the nurse was giving me in, and she saw "mammogram" and a plus sign, and she panicked.

"Oh my God, Dad!" she yelled out, and then, even more frantic, she screamed, "Oh my God! It's happening! Dad, get up here! You need to come up here now! Mom's test came back. Oh my God, it's happening again!" She was a frantic mess, screaming at my husband and pacing in front of me, and the whole time I was trying to keep her quiet so I could hear what was on the phone.

And that was how the journey began for all of us, and each of us went through our own moments or anger—anger from fear, anger from confusion, anger from desperation, and anger from frustration. Each new stage we came to, there was something that was maddening, and we wouldn't have been really dealing with the situation if we refused ourselves the right to be angry because the fact of the matter is, cancer is maddening. It's not fair. It hurts so many people, and it never tells you why. It comes into lives without asking and upends everything. It punishes us for crimes we never committed, and it takes entire families by storm, and in our case, it seemed to be working through our family. So anger was something I found that was absolutely a part of working to healing.

The diagnosis itself is shattering, and when it comes, so does the first bout of anger because everyone's immediate reaction is "I don't deserve this." And that's true; no one deserves this, and injustice is something to get angry about.

For me, the way cancer just invaded my body was an outrage. I felt like a Pac-Man had been let loose inside me and was just eating away at me. Even though they said it was a slow-growing breast cancer, it still felt like I had an intruder racing through my body trying to destroy me. To me it felt like an insatiable Pac-Man because a year ago it wasn't there, and then a year goes by and four spots show up. To me that was fast, and all

I wanted was for it to be out of my body because I had done nothing to let it in, so it had no business affecting me the way it was.

The thing about cancer that is probably the most maddening is the way that it touches so many parts of your life. After I began my treatments, I began to get angry because I felt I was being robbed of my former life. My schedule revolved around doctors' appointments and treatments, I couldn't sleep at night because of the medications, I was losing weight by the day and couldn't control it, and I could no longer even do housework the way I wanted. Because the chemo and the radiation were so draining, it was nearly impossible for me to do anything. Before cancer, I was a real neat freak. Once I started chemo, though, the housework had to be put on the backburner. I'd pick up the big chunks, dust the front of things, spray deodorizer so people presume it was clean, but I knew differently. I hate a messy house, but I had to overlook that while I was doing chemo. I just didn't have the energy like I used to. I would have every intention of doing some chores, but the couch would win every time.

Then there was what felt like constant loss for me. I lost my energy, I lost my breasts, and I lost my hair and eyelashes. With each step, I would feel a twinge of anger for my loss, but I also got through the anger and found something to be thankful for in the end. I couldn't have made it to gratitude, though, without the anger. This was a tough lesson for me, too, because I don't like to be angry. I thrive on positivity and feel that anger is often a wasted emotion. I now realize that anger is wasteful if we are consumed by it, but it is helpful if we move in and out of it quickly and use it as a stepping-stone to the next level rather than a permanent residence.

## MY DIAGNOSIS FROM ANOTHER POINT OF VIEW

It isn't just the patient who must work through anger, either. It's the family. My children, for example, experienced cancer from a very different angle, and they felt angry for different reasons, some of which I wasn't even aware of until the writing of this book.

Kira, unlike me, is a very tough, straightforward person. She is verbal and doesn't shy away from telling anyone what she is thinking. Because Kira is such a strong person, it was hard for her to deal with certain aspects of the journey, especially when she thought that either the doctors weren't moving fast enough or I wasn't being open enough. I had and have amazing doctors who always give me their all and walk me through the process every step of the way. The truth is, between my doctors and the different classes that hospitals set up just for cancer patients, I have been very well taken care of, but for a daughter who wants to be sure her mother will be there to watch her children become adults, it's sometimes near impossible to stay patient and not feel overwhelmed and angry at everyone involved in the cancer process, including doctors and the patient herself.

*Kitana & Myself*

Kira would find herself getting angry with me because she felt that I didn't speak up enough about things that were going on, pains and discomforts. She felt I had an aversion to feeling like I was the whiny patient but that I needed to get past that and tell the doctors about anything that was happening to me. Kira felt I had every right to stand up and say, "I want to be seen for this," or, "Hey, this is going on," or, "Can you help me?" She was frustrated that I didn't want to do that, and she had every right to feel that way because my life was intertwined with hers.

For Kira, there was even a bigger loss of control than there was for me in some ways because not only had cancer barged into her life, but she also couldn't control how treatment would go or what the doctors were told because it wasn't in her body. For her, because this was happening to her mom and children's grandmother, it never seemed that anyone was doing enough, but she couldn't do anything to change that. It's like torture to feel so out of control, and it's exasperating.

The only way one could avoid feeling angry at such an overwhelming situation would be to turn off emotionally and detach, and I have found personally from my experience with Beth that cutting ourselves off from a loved one with cancer will only cause more pain and regret, so we have to let ourselves be angry so we stay engaged.

———————

Ultimately, feeling angry after a diagnosis and even through the treatment process is nothing to feel ashamed of. Like fear, sadness, acceptance, hope, and joy, anger has its place in the process of healing and recovery. It keeps us involved and helps us to learn about our situation, and it also means that we are still engaged and putting up a fight, and that is something we always must do. So be angry, but just remember, don't linger there too long, keep your eyes forward, and realize that once you get past anger, healing is waiting on the other side. For me, on the other side of anger I realized that cancer might take a lot from us, but it can never take our souls.

# LESSON 4:

# TEARS OF HEALING

*Don't be afraid to cry. Tears are just water drops flowing down your face. They cleanse the soul. It's okay to mourn your loss...*

Before I started to experience real loss, I have to admit, I was somewhat of a closed-off person.

It wasn't that I withheld love from my family and friends, but I certainly was emotionally conservative as far as really opening up to others went. After both my mom and dad passed, though, I think that my siblings and I realized how important it is that we as their children stick together. That was a valuable lesson learned in the wake of so much sorrow.

Mom dying was hard on everyone, especially my dad, but when Dad died, there was a lot to deal with beyond death itself that brought our family together, the biggest of which was selling the farm.

Because Dad was the second to go and no one could afford it, we had to sell the place that we and our father had been raised on. Dad originally wanted to leave it to one of the boys, but no one could take it, or afford taking it, so we decided before Dad died that when it was time, we would divide everything up in the house among us and then sell the place.

Not long after we had the conversation, the day came that we had to say good-bye to Dad. On his death bed, he asked for my granddaughter, the one he took out first on the four-wheeler I'd convinced him to buy. After that, he was in and out of consciousness pretty much until he passed, but everyone sat around until he took his final breath.

The day before he passed, Dad sat in a recliner in the living room that we all gathered around as we sung and told stories. He looked up at one point and asked, "Where's my bald eagle?" Beth had just lost all her hair from the chemo treatments, and she showed the whole family her bald head for the first time, so Dad called her his bald eagle.

She just happened to come in when Dad said that. She started to cry and asked, "Somebody have a marker?" Someone handed her one, and she took it, walked over to Dad, and wrote "bald eagle" on his head. He looked up at her and said, "That wasn't very nice."

"I know," she said. "I'm not a nice girl. Now we're both bald eagles."

After Beth finished writing on Dad's head, it was his turn. He reached out and took the marker from her with the little energy he had and scribbled on her bald head too.

"Daddy, now we're both bald eagles," Beth said as she kneeled next to Dad.

At that point everyone started crying and laughing, and that was pretty much it. The crying and the laughing helped ease all our pains and fears. We all let ourselves experience the emotions that came up, and allowing that helped us work our way through it in a peaceful way. We didn't leave the room to cry or hold back. We just cried, and laughed, and it all carried us through.

My only fear during the entire time was that I'd have to be the one to make the call with the morphine. I was chosen to make the call when my mother had passed, so I knew it would land on me again. And I was right. I ended up giving him morphine. I knew I would push him over the edge to the point that breathing was not comfortable for life. For me that was the hardest, to have to give that morphine.

It was a beautiful death in the end, though. In fact, this was the first death I really experienced that was peaceful and everybody was happy. It was a whole new experience of somebody dying. It truly was a beautiful death.

Then came the funeral. All ten of us carried my dad's urn, and weeks later we went back to the house to split things up. It was comforting to be in his house after he passed. It was where so many of our memories lived. As we loaded up boxes, everybody was telling jokes and stories of the past. So it was like a comfortable place to come because my mom and dad were both there. It was almost like it connected to the heart again.

My oldest brother, to lighten things up, put on mom's lipstick. He did this when she died, too. There was something about that bright-pink lipstick that made him feel close and connected. So he put on the lipstick, and he passed the lipstick around and everybody else put it on.

As we did all this, we all let ourselves cry. It was then I began to learn how crying was cleansing and that it was a natural part of loss, even if the loss was peaceful and expected. I also learned that crying is a good indicator that we are dealing with our emotions. Tears are proof that we are allowing someone else in and all our fears, anxieties, and even hopes out for another to experience, or maybe just for us to fully experience all alone. And I had to remind myself of that again and again with one diagnosis after the next in my family.

Losing my parents was only a training course in tears for me. I still had a lot to learn about the many functions of tears, and Beth's diagnosis was my next lesson in crying. I didn't really understand it completely until I went through the process myself.

After Beth was diagnosed, I would take her to her appointments from time to time, so I was getting a glimpse at what life was like post-diagnosis, but I was still a little baffled by the whole thing. One thing that stood out in particular was her reaction to her last radiation treatment.

For her last radiation, I took Beth a gift bag because I knew it might be tough on her. I'd been doing these gift bags all along, and every time I'd throw something in pink. Every package I took her always had pink in it—in a pink bag or pink water bottle or pink wash-cloth, something pink that she could use for herself to enjoy her illness with. I thought it might make it easier, and it was always pink. I look back and think of how disgusted she must've been with pink. I would never do that again, but at the time I thought it would help, and when I gave her the gift basket with something pink for her last radiation treatment, I was shocked by her response.

We got to the car, and I handed it to her, and she just burst out in tears. She bawled all the way back home. For two weeks after that she was an emotional wreck. No one had any idea what to do or even why she was so upset. This should've been a joyous occasion for her. She got rid of one doctor; she was over that step.

"Why is this so traumatic for you?" I asked as she wept.

"No, you just don't understand," she said. "I feel this emptiness, like whose gonna take care of me now?"

I said, "What do you mean? They're done taking care of you. Why are you doing this? Why are you feeling like this?"

At the time, I just chalked all the crying up to her personality. She had a sentimental side to her, and I figured it was just taking over. Or maybe it was the medication. *It has to be something,* I thought, *because there is no reason to cry over your last radiation treatment.* Then I went through radiation myself.

As I was going through radiation, one day when I went in for a treatment there was another lady in the bathroom, and as we were standing and washing our hands, she suddenly turned to me and said, "It's my last radiation day," and she started crying.

"That's a good thing," I said, trying to comfort her. "You should be happy about it."

"I know I should be happy." She sobbed. "I don't know what it is, like an emptiness. Who's going to take care of me now?"

I thought, *Oh my gosh, this is almost like a roller coaster that everybody goes through some time or another.*

Suddenly doctors are starting to be taken out of your life. You're feeling like you're in a cave for a very long time, and somebody's taking care of you, and all of a sudden, now what? Where do I go? And so now you're just feeling like you're on your own, like there's nobody out there for you anymore, so all you can do to handle the feeling is cry, and that is okay because sometimes there just isn't any other way to handle something so overwhelming. Once we get our crying out, though, there's something that washes over us and makes us feel fresh again. It's like we've cried the overwhelming feeling out of us somehow.

Standing, looking at that women with bloodshot eyes and her face soaked in tears, I began to see that tears were just a way to get to the next level. If I thought about it, it was how I'd handled every step of the way myself, from the time I found out and every step after that; tears helped me figure everything out.

When I was first told the results of biopsies, my heart sank. Tears filled my eyes that day as I stood in the kitchen and scribbled down all the information the nurse was giving me. There in front of my daughter and husband, I cried because suddenly my health had been taken from me, and I needed to mourn that loss.

In the days following, there was this helpless feeling I couldn't shake, and the wait and wondering only made it worse. I would be fine and then suddenly be overwhelmed with a feeling of dread and fear and sadness. I felt like I had endured a death. It hit me hard. I'd be driving home from work and just burst into a sobbing fit that was so intense the tears blinded me. You try to stay positive and pull every ounce of life out of what you have left to play with, but sometimes it is really hard. Sometimes there are many roadblocks and you just have to let yourself cry.

After the biopsies, I had yet another major hurdle to get past: my bilateral mastectomy. When I first got my results back, the doctor told me that they found invasive receptor cancer.

"It skipped the first lymph node altogether and showed up in the second," he explained. "We've never

had that before." Since my first biopsies were cancelled, they were not sure if there was any cancer in my
right breast.

That meant we had no choice but to do a bilateral mastectomy, so I would have both of my breasts
removed. I remember when my sister was going through
this, I talked to my regular doctor and I said, "Oh my
God, there's no way I could lose my breast. I think I
would have a problem with that." I had never been big-
busted, but breasts are a major part of femininity, and I
would not have an easy time just getting rid of them. I
knew that I wanted the cancer gone, though.

Since all this had started, Duane kind of internal-
ized a lot. He wouldn't talk to me about it, but he would
talk to Kira. I think he probably wanted to stay strong
for me, but he was also just a reserved person where
emotions were concerned. And then Brad, he was the
shy one. He's like me; he internalizes everything. Then
all of a sudden he would burst out in tears, and nobody
would ever know that he was even sad. I was glad that
he learned to use his tears, though, since he was so
introverted. It wasn't just good for him, but it let us
know how he was really feeling.

On the morning of the surgery, we got to the hospital,
and a lot of my family was there. As I hugged everyone and thanked them for coming (I'd started to hug a
lot more since I'd lost my parents), I could tell Duane
was scared. He was wringing his hands quite a bit and
seemed fidgety. I knew what was going through his
head: he thought I was going to die.

I tried to calm his nerves. I kept telling him, "I am not going to die. I'm coming back up. I'll be out, and I'll see you in about four to five hours." I tried to reassure him, but he'd always disappear to a part of the room, and I knew it was to go cry. I wanted to tell him that it was okay to cry—that it was natural and that I'd been doing a lot of it, too.

I want to tell everyone who is going through this, whether personally or with a family member, that crying is okay, and it helps us heal. He wasn't ready yet, I guess, to let me see him cry, and I understood.

The surgery went well, but coming out of it I was pretty groggy. I don't remember hardly anybody being there other than Duane. When I opened my eyes, he was sitting at my bedside. He held my wedding ring for me during the surgery, and when I came to, he took my hand and said, "Jeanne."

"What?" I asked.

At that moment, I saw a tear roll down his cheek, and he said, "Will you marry me?"

"Oh yeah, I will marry you. Again and again and again I will marry you."

He put the ring on my finger and gave me a kiss, and then he started crying again and went back out. Duane did eventually start to cry in front of me. Of course, it was heartbreaking to me every time, but I try to remember that I'm not the only one going through this and that he needs to be able to cleanse his own mind from time to time.

## MY DIAGNOSIS FROM ANOTHER POINT OF VIEW

Kira saw a real change in her dad after I was diagnosed with breast cancer, and although I can't say that I wish the reason for the change didn't exist, I can say I am glad that it has happened. To Kira, she got to see a side of her dad that she never knew about, even more than I did since Duane would often disclose all his feelings to her more than anyone else.

After dealing with cancer, Kira saw her father not as more emotional, as he'd always been a loving dad, but as more compassionate. Before, she saw him as a man who held back tears and did his best not to show any emotions, but after my diagnosis, she noticed that he didn't hold back his tears anymore. She said, "He's not gonna hide from anything. If he wants to cry, he'll cry." Kira felt that my cancer diagnosis made him realize that there was no reason to hold back.

---

Facing the cancer demon is tough, and it's easy to lose sight of the lessons we are able to learn when we are battling it. Often, I found myself trying to avoid it, but I turn around and there it is. Going back to work was particularly hard because, as a respiratory therapist, I see a lot of others fighting the same fight as me. I see people my age and younger who I can tell have cancer because of their pale skin or because they have no hair, and suddenly I have to deal with my own illness all over again. And the loss of a cancer client always tugs at my heart in a way it never used to. When it all gets to be too much, I have a few good cleansing cries. I let myself mourn the loss.

So, along with so many others, learning to cry and how to use my tears has been a valuable lesson that my family and I have taken from my journey. I think it was a lesson that we probably all needed to learn since we were all guarded in our own ways. I think that most people are guarded in their own ways. To many, fighting the tears that are welling up in our eyes is usually our instinct, but I have learned that when we let those tears lose, we are also letting go of a little bit of the pain we are holding. Those tears aren't just a physical reaction to something; they are a means of moving through a tough time. We shouldn't fear our tears; we should allow them to do their jobs, which is to cleanse our souls.

Once I began to let myself use my tears to heal, I began to feel more peace. I started to see that things can change, that my emotions and outlook could change, if I let myself go through the process. I came to see these changes as colors. What is my color now? Today I feel:

Pink= power in numbers. Fight for life and don't give up.

Blue=inner calmness, sense of worth.

Brown= well grounded. I know what's important to me in life. I'm at peace in my own body.

*Duane and me*

*My Family: Duane, Kira, Brad, and myself*

*Sporting a kiss in Mommy's favorite lipstick after head shaving party*

*Brother Mike lightening the mood with Mommy lipstick*

*My little "Monkey-Shine," Kitana finger painting my bald head*

# LESSON 5:

# COURAGE IS OPTIONAL

*You don't have to be strong by yourself. Use other people for your strength.*

When you're diagnosed with cancer, you suddenly get bombarded with a lot at once, and there's just no way to take it all in without a support system to help you. I think for a lot of people, a cancer diagnosis feels like something the diagnosed needs to protect their loved ones from. In reality, though, when you're diagnosed with cancer, you need your loved ones to help you get through it, and you are not a weak person for using all the support that the people around you can offer.

Through my own journey, I have found that courage comes easier in numbers, so the best thing you can do is let the people you love help you fight the fight. Beth actually introduced me to that notion, but I still had some learning to do on my own before I really understood completely.

When everything first started, Duane and I decided that we wouldn't tell the kids yet. We did tell Beth, but I made her swear to secrecy that she wouldn't say anything to the rest of the family. We told her just before we went in for the first biopsy surgery, and she swore not to say a word to anyone. Her husband walked in as we were discussing everything and asked what was going on, so we told him but made him give his word he wouldn't say anything either.

After I had my first biopsies scheduled, Beth had a gathering of the siblings at their farmhouse's garage to discuss what we'd do when Dad passed away. She took control of the situation—worked out the responsibilities as to who was going to do what when Dad was gone. I thought it was strange how the sickest one took it upon herself to be the responsible one in the family, but that was Beth. She is a strong-willed person, and she seems to approach whatever life throws at her head-on. While we were having this little meeting, Beth walked over to me and handed me a letter.

"I want you to read this," she told me. I knew that since Beth started chemo it was hard for her to sleep, so she'd been journaling a lot. I figured it was something she'd written to all of us on one of her sleepless nights, so I agreed without looking at what it said before I started.

"I have a secret. I found a lump," I said, reading the letter line by line in front of all my siblings.

As soon as it came out of my mouth, I was furious. Beth had set me up. My eyes shot over to where she was standing, and I glared at her through the tears that glazed my eyes. *I can't believe you're telling everybody this. I can't believe you broke our secret*, I thought as I glared at her.

It didn't take long for the tears to make their way from the corners of my eyes to my cheeks. So I stood there, shocked at what my sister had done, and crying. I was so mad at her that I couldn't read the rest of the letter.

"Jeanne," she said when she saw what was happening. "Stop and just read the rest of the letter." I couldn't believe the nerve she had.

*I can't believe you broke our secret in front of my whole family, and you didn't even tell me you were going to do this*, I snapped silently inside my head.

Beth seemed unaffected by my seething anger, and she just repeated, "Jeanne, stop. You need to read the letter."

Despite my anger, I wiped my tears aside and started to read the letter again. As I recited what was on the page, one word after the next, I realized she hadn't tricked me at all. What I was reading wasn't a confession of my own; it was her story, which became mine for a little bit. It became all of ours.

As I read on, my pulse slowed, my anger subsided, and suddenly the mood in the room had completely changed. We went into this happy little party in the garage, and it all started with Beth's letter—the letter that shared her story and allowed her story to become ours. In her ability to let others in, she had found some strength and some peace. I started to see then how much easier it is to face something so scary as a team, and that is what I started to do too.

On November 9, my doctor set up an oncology appointment for me. The doctor told me the appointment could last up to three hours. We would discuss the chemo path, also known as a chemo map, during that time. I hadn't a clue what any of that meant, but I knew that all the appointments were going to be overwhelming at best and terrifying at worst, so I asked Duane and Kira to join me—strength in numbers.

Prior to all this, I had just assumed that I would understand the bulk of what was said, regardless of how daunting it might be. I figured that working in the medical field myself, I would know a lot of the terms and recognize a lot of the stuff the oncologist would be telling me. I was sorely mistaken.

Within the first fifteen minutes with the oncologist, I glazed over. I still can't remember much of anything the doctor said to me that day. I just stared at his mouth as it opened and closed. It was like I was watching a foreign film all of a sudden. It wasn't that I was *trying* to block him out; I just could not make sense of anything he said; after the word *cancer*, I went blank. I thought, *I hope Duane and Kira are getting some of this*, as I sat and watched the doctor's hands tap his desk and his fingers glide over diagrams he had spread out in front of us. I watched him closely, but I heard nothing at all that he said. The entire appointment seemed so confrontational, so I just kind of went away.

Something that I did catch in that first appointment was the gist of how chemo was going to work. I'd have four treatments, three weeks apart. Then I'd have a PET scan to find out if there was anything else going on in my body; the scans were from head to toe. They also set up chemo classes, which were mandatory. I would have to go through that before I even started chemo.

The doctor also explained I would have to do a radiation consult to plan a radiation schedule, so when we were done with the chemo we could move on to the next step.

I would have expanders, which are part of reconstruction. These go under your pectoral muscles to expand for the breast implant when the time comes, so special care had to be taken for that. It was all so exhausting. When the consultation finally ended, I felt like I'd run a marathon I was so drained, and I still hardly had any idea what was going on.

I couldn't have made it through even the consultations without my husband and daughter there, not only to help me catch what I missed but also because their simple presence made me feel like I wasn't doing this alone. I felt like, at the very least, I had people on my side that were going to help me get through this, and I needed all the support I could get because I could already tell that there was a lot to the cancer game.

After the consultations came my pathology report, which was also pretty intimidating. My plastic surgeon explained to me that first they would hollow out the breast and then take out the nipple, since the nipple is part of the carrier of cancer usually.

They cleared out the twelve lymph nodes on the left and six on the right. There were no cancer cells on the right side, but there was a large amount of cancerous cells on the left, and if they were left alone without any radiation, their chances of producing cancer were pretty high, so they opted do radiation with that too.

Everything seemed even more confusing for me because they hadn't really had a case like mine. The cancer skipped the first lymph node and went straight to the second, which made it a special case altogether. My cancer was also noncontained, or spreading all over in different spots, so things were difficult for a number of reasons. Then they had the expanders in there, so they weren't really sure what to do with my radiation treatment. My radiologist did some calling around and got a second and third opinion on what to do for my case, so it would seem that even experienced doctors were a little confused by my treatment.

While the doctor was getting second and third opinions, Kira and I were going through chemo class together. I couldn't even imagine doing that alone. At first I thought bringing someone along who didn't have cancer to sit through a chemo class was a bit strange, but once I got there, I felt like Kira was my lifesaver. She kept my head above the water.

The class started at eight in the morning and lasted three hours. I think I was the youngest one in there. The rest were older, but they also had a little support system with them. Together Kira and I learned loads of information about what chemo does and what things people undergoing treatment should do. They explained how we needed to keep our bladders empty; otherwise the chemo could cause a breakdown in the bladder. The thing that stands out most to me is something they said about always using condoms after chemo so it doesn't come into contact with your spouse.

"Did you hear that, Mom?" Kira leaned over and whispered to me out of the corner of her mouth, nudging me with her elbow. "This is important. You need to listen to this. You need to wear a condom," she teased.

"Oh. Kira," I said, rolling my eyes a little. "I don't think that will be a problem. Dad and I are more to the mental part of our relationship. It doesn't have to be sex all the time anymore. We're past all that."

She shrugged and flashed a quick smile. "Oh, well, you better write that down just in case."

I had a little medical book I kept with me since the diagnosis, and Kira grabbed it and wrote "*Use Condoms*" in it with all the other important things we were learning.

We weren't the only ones tickled by the idea of going back to using condoms. I mentioned I was the youngest there, so there were people in their seventies getting lectured about safe sex and using protection all over again (of course this was a kind of "safe sex" none of us had ever even imagined). I looked around the room the second I heard "condom," and everyone was giggling, save one person who had his ears closed. It was like being at sex-ed in junior high, all of us chuckling at the word *condom*. I think we all really appreciated that little laugh though. We needed it because next came the hard part: side effects.

They went through the seven-mile list of awful things chemo might do to us, how chemo was going to happen, and how often it would be. There would be four treatments, and they would take eight hours. We would have blood work and see a provider after that. We'd be put on a steroid to help with all the side effects, which were plenty. We were going to have huge reactions and get sick. We needed to flush twice and be sure to void as soon as we could.

There was so much to take in at once, and at times I wanted to shut off because I almost didn't *want* to hear about how all these terrible chemicals were going to destroy my body. Ignorance is bliss, you know? I didn't know how much I could take, so it was beyond helpful to have Kira sitting by my side, writing furiously when I needed to take a break from all of it mentally.

After three hours of chemo training, I was ready for the next step, a PET scan. For this, a patient is injected with radioactive tracers and then sits for forty-five minutes all alone. There can be no noise at all. You can't even read while you're sitting there. Any noise or reading could cause a bad scan. The PET scan allows the doctors to see how the tissues and organs in your body are actually functioning.

My granddaughter, Kitana, and Kira came with me for the test, and I had to tell them they couldn't come in with me. I just had to sit in a dark room all by myself, with no magazines, and I had a migraine on top of it from fasting all night. It was a disappointment not to have my little support system with me in the room, but it was nice to have them before and after. Kira told me later that Kitana didn't handle driving away from the clinic that day very well at all. She cried, "We can't leave Grandma, Mom! We can't just leave her!" When

I heard that, it warmed and broke my heart at the same time. Who knew a three-year-old could be such a support for someone in her forties?

After that was my port, which is where they connect and administer chemo. Mine was on my upper chest, just below my right clavicle area. I had the surgery for that and was off work for a few days recovering. When they were finished, I looked at this new thing on my body. It was like a little lump under my skin. It seemed like I was losing and getting new things all the time since my diagnosis. My body was becoming quite foreign to me, but that too I would deal with in due time.

With the classes and surgeries and port placement behind us, I was ready for the big show: chemotherapy. I started chemo on November 17. I still really didn't know what chemo was, but the time had come, so I would be doing it regardless of my understanding of it.

Duane decided he would be with me for the eight hours I did the chemo. The first day we went in and sat in this the room. They brought in an IV pole and told me to go to the bathroom then so I wouldn't be up and down.

"Plan on an eight-hour day," the nurse said as she hooked me up.

And so we did. We sat in this little tiny room—it was probably only about ten feet by ten feet—and I was hooked to an IV. I thought, *Oh, so this is chemo. Just a drip from my IV bag.* I remember my sister saying that chemo was this red liquid going into her veins and she knew it was going to kill her. I had this terrifying fear from what my sister told me about her chemo treatments, but mine wasn't red, and I watched very closely as it neared my veins with fear, but I didn't feel a thing when it started to hit my veins. When it went in, I felt nothing. So I did all my Christmas cards and thank-yous, and I thought, *This isn't bad like my sister said it was going to be.* I actually found it to be kind of peaceful, like a break from the chaos of life.

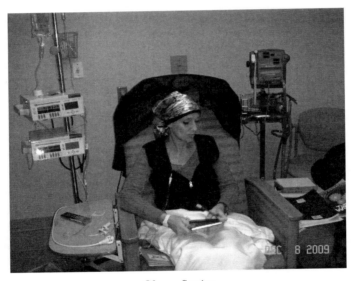

*Chemo Session*

I decided that I could handle this whole chemo thing. I came to the realization that I could be scared and fret about how horrible it was or take my own oath to be strong and optimistic and make my own route. We all have demons that we fear in our lives, and I thought that for me chemo would not be one. I would take this and do it as gracefully and elegantly as I possibly could. I would show people how chemo and radiation were done and that you didn't have to feel like you were dying because you were doing it. I thought, *Okay, that empowers me. I'm going to use that, and I'm going to carry on through these treatments and do what I need to do. I'm going to speak for people and be their voice.*

So I did the best I could with the cards I was dealt, and I used chemo treatments as a way to get closer to my husband. I did the steroids two times a day before and after chemo. They gave me Compazine for nausea and did what they could to keep me as comfortable as possible. Duane and I started looking at it as a date. We'd spend eight hours in this little room, just him and me. I'd have chemo, and we'd talk, get caught up in our reading, and all the good stuff we never had a chance to do. Because I had Duane there with me, chemo became less threatening and more precious; it was time with the person I loved most in the world.

Doing the chemo never seemed so bad to me. I wasn't working while I did it, so not only did I get an eight-hour date with Duane, but every day my grand-daughter, Kitana, was at my house, brightening my spirits. She was my little savior; she was three years old, and she kept me going. Being a toddler, she was nonjudgmental about everything. She knew something was wrong, but she approached everything just the right way.

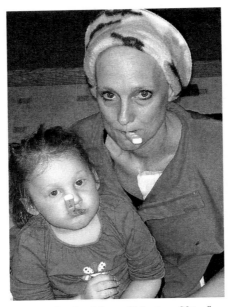

*"Sick Bay" with my "Monkey-Shine"*

Every once in a while, she would ask me, "Oh, Grandma, do you hurt?" and she'd do what she could to soothe me.

Things started to get intense after a couple of sessions, though. I had every side effect in the book plus three. Weight was dropping off me, I hurt all over, and I couldn't stand the smell of food. It seemed like every day something new came up. I had neuropathy, problems with my bladder, and at times I felt like my insides were being torn from my body, but I had Kitana there by my side to be strong when I felt like I couldn't.

My granddaughter of all people reminded me that I could do this when I felt like I was hitting rock bottom, in her little three-year-old way. Children are the most sincere people on the planet, so her encouragement meant the world because it came without judgment or pretense. We all need that when we're going through something so severe. I think I may have sunk without her sometimes, without everyone who helped me up when I felt my strength faltering.

She'd help put the bandages on for me and tried to take a little peek. It was almost like she was my little nurse. She would lay on the couch with me and we'd watch movies. When my hair would start to pop up in little spikes after it had all fallen out, she would say, "Oh, Grandma, your hair is starting to grow back! You can take your hat off! You don't have to be embarrassed anymore!"

It was almost like she knew what I was going through. She was like a grown-up in a tiny little body, and she helped me pull through every stage—through the exhaustion, the sickness, the hair loss, and all the other physical changes. My little granddaughter was my anchor through it all. I learned how to take life lightly from Kitana. Now I listen from a new level since my diagnosis, and she helped me learn how to do that.

## MY DIAGNOSIS FROM ANOTHER POINT OF VIEW

I learned quickly how cancer is not something that you tackle alone. I didn't just happen upon that realization, either. There was Beth, of course, but Kira also made that abundantly clear from the very second I found out that I had breast cancer.

The day that the doctor's office called me with my biopsy results and said they were positive, Kira was there. I've said how she and Duane were in the basement and she came up as I was on the phone. I also said how her first reaction was to kind of panic for a second or two, but I haven't finished that story yet.

It didn't take Kira more than a minute or two to move from shock to action. As soon as I hung up the phone, she was ready to make a game plan to conquer this diagnosis. She has always been strong, so it shouldn't have surprised me, but still I was a little amazed by her take-charge attitude.

Instead of breaking down, Kira started strategizing. Her thoughts were, *Okay, we need to come up with a plan. That's all there is to do now, plan.*

"This isn't going to take your life," she said to me very matter-of-factly as we were all sitting around our dining room table. "We need to find a way to get through all of this together."

Kira wasn't going to think about anything but the fight, and she knew that we were going to have to support each other to win it. Her focus was solely on how we needed to figure out something, because she knew that if we didn't make a plan of action, winning the fight was out of the question.

"We're going to have to be strong in turns," she said. "We can't all be down at the same time."

Cancer is awful, but it can do some magical things at the same time. For me, cancer showed me how strong my little girl really was. It also showed me how wise she was. Kira realized from the start that this was going to be a real battle for us all, but there had to always be at least one of us carrying the torch throughout the process.

It was like she had already jumped into the thick of it and could see what was ahead because she was absolutely right, and tackling cancer as a team was the only way we got through. When one person went down, the other would pull him or her back up to the surface. This didn't just keep the ship from sinking; it let each of us experience the stages we needed to get us to the other side.

I don't know how she did it, but Kira knew that what we were about to take on would require all of us working together and fighting in shifts. For Kira, my diagnosis was just an obstacle that we needed to overcome as a family.

*Daughter, Kira, and me*

It was a problem that had to be solved, and there was power in numbers as far as finding a resolution was concerned. She knew that it would be daunting, but she also knew we'd get through if, and only if, we did it as a team.

---

I could never make it through everything without the support system around me. And everyone contributed in their own ways. Kira was more aggressive in her approach, taking me to appointments and even calling doctors when she felt things weren't right.

Then there was my son, Brad, who was more silent in his support. Brad is by nature more introverted than Kira, but his presence was what sometimes carried me through. He may not have said much, but he would be sure to simply be there, in the room, to let me know I was never alone.

*Son, Brad, and me*

For him, finding out his mom had cancer was shattering; he went through stages of shock, disbelief, anger, and sadness, but he did it more by himself than with others. That is just Brad. But even though he kept things to himself, he still supported me in his way, which was as important to me as anything else. Brad had a quiet voice, and he didn't want to intrude on something that could be so vulnerable for a female (breasts), but he always wanted to know how I was feeling, which let me know he was there for me. That's the thing about working as a team; everyone has their own roles, and every role is as important as the next. It is the different ways that a support system pulls together that makes it work.

Of course, it wasn't just Duane, Kira, and Brad who helped me to be courageous. My grandkids, my siblings, friends, all medical staff, and coworkers all gave little bits of themselves to me when I needed it most. The cancer may have been in *my* body, but everyone was fighting it, and I know that without all those people, I may not have been able to do it at times.

So my lesson here is this: beating cancer is a team effort. It takes a lot of courage, and it is going to be a struggle sometimes, but you never have to do it alone, and you never should try. God has put people in your life for a reason, so be sure that you let them play the role they were intended to play. When your courage and optimism is running low, let someone help you shoulder the burden while you get your strength back up.

# LESSON 6:

# DON'T TURN AWAY A GIFT FROM SOMEONE WANTING TO GIVE

*When you tell someone "no thanks" or "you didn't have to do that," you are taking away their right to help you. Allow people to assist and contribute because sometimes that is all they know to do.*

It is probably pretty clear by now that I am not the kind of person who feels comfortable accepting help from others. I've explained how that quality was both learned and inherited. My own mother died rather than putting someone out (as she saw it) by asking for help or complaining. That was just how she lived; it was everyone else first, and she couldn't find it in herself to ask anyone for anything. Her death alone spoke volumes to me, but my own battle with cancer has forced me to really get over any ideas I had about accepting help from others. Like so many other lessons, I saw this first in Beth but still needed some coaxing to accept it.

Beth seemed to handle certain things about her diagnosis with so much more ease than I did. I talk about Beth so much because she did everything just a year before me, so she was kind of my gauge through it all. And when Beth found out about her cancer, she just got out there and told everybody about it. With her, it was no secret.

"I've got cancer," she'd say to someone. "Do you wanna feel it?" She would actually even let people feel the lump before it was removed; women, of course. I had a hard time just telling people, and she would let people *feel* it.

Unlike me, Beth wasn't shy about anything when it came to her battle. She put the word out there, and all her friends got together and started bringing casseroles and lasagnas—meals on wheels we called it. Everybody brought a dinner one day a week for the family so she wouldn't have to cook. Beth's motto was to surround herself with tons of family and friends so it would not be so devastating on her children.

She had people coming and bringing things to her and giving her rides to the doctor's office; she even had friends going into the actual appointments with her and being a part of the whole experience. One friend would go to an appointment and write down what the doctor would say; the next friend would go to chemo or radiation with her. I remember the first time *I* went to radiation with her.

"Come on in," she said to me as we walked into the radiation room. "I want to introduce you to the workers."

It was so insane to me. She seemed almost at home in all this, like cancer was a source of pride for her in the way she shared it with others. I thought, *I don't think I would act like that. I think I would be afraid of the next step.* But for her, it was almost like showing someone a new purse.

I admit now I thought Beth was handling things, I don't know if I'd say wrong, but in a way that cancer was not supposed to be handled. I didn't get how she could just delegate things out to different people the way she did with the cooking of meals and the doctors' appointments. I thought it was just some quirk, the way she was going about things, but what I found out was Beth was just lucky that she could see from the get-go how to approach things. She knew that she would need help and couldn't see any reason not to ask. She trusted that her friends and family were more than willing to be there, and she let them. Beth's emotional support from friends and family was very strong, and the meals and supplies were a bonus. Beth started early building her army to protect her family.

For me, it took real effort to finally breakdown and see how unfair and unrealistic it was for me to refuse help or feel guilty about receiving it. I was a nervous wreck from the word *go* when it came to telling people and asking for anything. It started with my job.

When I first found out about my cancer and the treatment it would require, I immediately thought about how this was going to affect my work. I instantly felt guilty about it because I knew I was going to need a lot of time off for surgery and recovery. I had no idea how I was going to tell my supervisor, Peggy, or how she would take the news. I approached it in this really weird way, like I had done something wrong by having been diagnosed with cancer, and I felt awful asking for anyone to facilitate me and "my" problem. That is obviously not the way to go about things, but at first it is what I did.

Terrified of what was going to happen once I told my boss about my illness, I swallowed the fear back that was almost keeping me from breathing and made one of the many difficult phone calls I had to make post-diagnosis.

"This is Peggy."

My stomach twisted up into a tight knot as soon as she answered.

"Hi, Peggy," I said, trying to keep my voice even and cool. "Hey, can I meet with you?"

"Yeah, Jeanne," she said. "Are you okay?"

I just ignored that question and went on. "Can we meet in the front lobby?" I asked. "I don't wanna see anybody in my department. I just wanna meet with you, somewhere in private."

Peggy set up a spot where we could meet, a tiny little waiting room in the front of the building that had two chairs. She was already sitting in one of them when I came in.

I'm sure that I looked like a wreck. Duane was also with me for support, so I imagine she had some idea that what I had to say was not good. I tried to force a quick smile as I walked over to sit in the empty chair, but I couldn't keep myself from falling apart.

I sat down, and I started bawling. Duane stood above me and put his hand on my shoulder. I looked up at him, hoping that he would take that as a cue to tell her for me. Duane's head dropped, and I could see tears start to fall off the tip of his nose. He couldn't do it either.

"Jeanne, what is it?" Peggy asked, leaning in closer to me.

"Well," I said as I sniffed hard and tried to keep my tears at bay, "I need to take some vacation. It's not planned. It's urgent," I said, doing all I could not to break into a sobbing fit again. She was the first person outside my family I had told, so it was making everything so real. Peggy sat quietly and nodded as I continued.

"I really don't know when it's going to happen," I went on, "but I need some time off, I'm thinking the end of September or October."

"Okay," she said in a real hushed voice. "Anything."

For whatever reason, that set me off. I just blurted, "I've got breast cancer."

I tried taking deep breathes between sentences, but it was too much. Something had been broken open inside me, and deep breathing wasn't going to close it back up. I continued talking while I wept there in front of my boss in that tiny waiting room that was empty except for the three of us.

"I don't know how much time I'll need," I said, "but I think I need probably eight weeks of healing time."

"That's fine," she said in a sweet, assuring tone. "Whatever it is, you take it. You deal with it. Whatever you need, we'll work with it."

So she went up and took me off the schedule. I was scheduled for surgery October 20, and I worked up until October 18.

The day before the surgery I started to think of everything that would need to be done. I knew I needed to prepare meals for my family because they're not cooks. All I could think was that if I didn't do something, they'd probably eat fast food every day. I also cleaned the house from one end to the other. I liked the house to be spotless, and I knew I'd be out of commission, so I cleaned nonstop for the entire day almost. I never once thought about calling someone to help with any of it, and I exhausted myself trying to make sure everything was set for my downtime.

I went in and had my surgery and came out about six hours later and started the first part of reconstruction. I remember waking up in my room, and I looked up to see a doctor at my bedside talking to me. It was my plastic surgeon, and she had a sweet, soft voice as she gently touched my arm. I remember she said that things went well, but other than that I don't remember anything.

I went home from the hospital two days later because the H1N1 flu was so bad that they didn't allow visitors. The first day I had the surgery, I was allowed visitors, but they didn't allow anybody after that for fear of patients and visitors getting the flu. So just two days after my surgery, I was headed home.

I felt like some kind of creature from an alien movie when I left the hospital. I had these three tubes coming out of me, one on the right and two on the left, that they put in to help drain the fluid to prevent infection. Two of the drains I got to take out in just a week, but one had to stay because there was still drainage.

I was tender and couldn't do a lot of housework; there was no lifting my arms, so a lot of things were impossible for me. Kira was very protective the whole time. She wouldn't let me drive places to go pay bills or go to the post office. I felt some stress sitting as the passenger—as my daughter drove me from stop to stop, unwilling to let me drive myself. It was like she had become *my* mother.

Although it was hard for me from time to time to feel so helpless, I am grateful for all her compassion and also her dedication to me. Duane would also call on the phone to check in on me and give the kids orders not to let Mom lift, drive, or work. I'm so grateful for my family's consideration and for all their help. I only wish I would have been able to accept it more readily.

I feel like I may have wasted time and energy not just letting others help. I tried my hardest to do my own chores so that I wouldn't feel helpless. I could feel the strings of muscles that had been separated and repositioned, especially in my left side, every time I tried to vacuum or pick up the house. How many times do you use your arms in a day?

I wasn't supposed to lift anything more than three pounds. I had to take laundry out of the washer one piece at a time. I was putting sheets on the bed once, and I almost passed out from the pain. I lifted the mattress to get the fitted sheet under, and my left side felt like it had ripped open. I became faint and laid down;

then I felt like throwing up. It was too much, and I wasn't doing anyone any favors by not allowing someone to help.

I spent twelve weeks at home recovering, but after twelve weeks, I had to return, so it was back to work as radiation started. Work was a little tougher than I thought, not only because of the physical strain but because I felt like a different person returning. I wasn't the Jeanne that had left my coworkers. I was the new *bald* Jeanne who was fighting cancer and might not be as capable as before. I was scared to death of what people would think of me.

The first day back I couldn't just walk in alone, so Peggy met me outside, and we walked in together. As we were making our way to our floor, I started crying. We were in an empty hallway, and I just lost it.

"What's the matter, Jeanne?" Peggy asked as she came to halt.

"Oh my God," I sobbed, "I feel so vulnerable. I don't know if I can do this. I don't know if I can come back."

"Jeanne, stop it," she said firmly.

I stopped crying for a second and looked at her. I thought, *Well, you're not very supportive.*

"Stop it," she said again, as forcefully as before. "People want to help you. They want to work with you. They've been looking forward to you coming back. You just need to stop it."

I gathered myself, and I said to myself, *Okay, I'm going to do this with grace and ease, like I keep saying I am. Wow, this is really hard.*

It wasn't an easy ride, but Peggy was right, people wanted me back. They were glad to have me back. Sure, there were some stares, and I won't say I didn't catch a doctor's jaw drop when he saw me for the first time, hairless and thinner than I was before, but overall, people there wanted to be there for me, and they showed it when it really counted.

---

Cancer is not cheap. It doesn't just cost a lot in doctors' bills and treatments, but also time away from work. Between the surgeries and the sickness, work is sometimes not an option. Unfortunately bills don't stop coming just because you have breast cancer, so you can find yourself in a tough spot really fast where money is concerned. Duane and I certainly did, and I had no idea what we'd do to survive, but then something amazing happened.

My boss and coworkers got together and donated their own vacation and sick leave to cover my time away so I wouldn't lose any more income while I was out. I couldn't believe it when I heard.

"Jeanne," Peggy said, "I have a little good news for you."

"I need some," I told her. I had to take off more time than I anticipated, and I knew we couldn't afford it.

"I knew that you didn't have any more leave, and I know that all this costs a lot, so we sent around an e-mail and asked if anyone could donate some time, and I think we have you covered for a few more weeks."

"What?" I said. I couldn't believe it. "You guys didn't have to do that," I told Peggy.

"No, we didn't," Peggy said. "We *wanted* to."

I requested a list later of all the people who had donated time. I was overwhelmed with gratitude as I sat and read it. Most of the people I didn't even know, and they gave up their time off to help me. These people who didn't even know me and wanted absolutely nothing in return were willing to just give up their own vacation to help me. I was absolutely moved, and it hit me all at once.

## My Diagnosis from Another Point of View

I was so worried about being a burden after my surgeries that I failed to see that my resistance was more taxing than my need for help, especially for Kira, as she was with me the most after my surgeries. I didn't want her to feel like she had to take time out of her life to chauffer me around all day, so I missed the glaring fact that Kira *wanted* to be there to help.

My pride kept me from seeing that being there to help me actually made Kira feel a little better about what was happening because she was doing her part to help me beat this.

Thank God Kira is as assertive as she is. No matter how much I insisted I would be fine or how much I pleaded with her to go about her life, she wouldn't hear of it. She didn't care about her spare time; she cared about me, and I was making that difficult at times when I resisted her.

What I didn't understand at the time was that Kira didn't view me as a burden at all. Her outlook on it was she was doing for me what I had done for her the last couple of decades. If I would've just let her tell me how she felt instead of assuming, Kira would have told me this:

"Don't ever feel through all this that you can't ask for help. I will be here for you every step of the way, just as you have been for me for the last twenty-five years. As long as you promise me that you will fight and *keep* fighting! I love you!"

---

How could I continue on in life and not call upon people to help? I had never taken from people before, so it was tough at first, and still is, but I now see that to receive is an amazing gift, not just to the recipient but to the giver. Those offering help truly wish to give, and if I reject it, it is like saying their gift is not worthy. I wasn't raised to be a taker, but I needed to get over that because I wasn't "taking." I was "receiving."

At first, every time someone brought something, I would try to find some way to repay them. Finally one day I stared into the mirror for about half an hour and found my soul, my identity from within myself, and my emotions that connect to my heart. *Wow*, how powerful.

I came to the realization that it wasn't my place to turn people away who were trying to help. It wasn't fair for them or for me to be stubborn and say, "No, thank you." Rejecting the gifts that people offered was kind of like rejecting them, like telling them their gift wasn't precious to me. My rejection made me seem ungrateful, and I was anything but ungrateful, so I learned to accept what was given and to appreciate it (even though you may be uneasy about it) instead of turning it away or feeling guilty. People want to help, so let them.

# LESSON 7:

# LET GO OF WHO YOU THINK YOU ARE AND LEARN TO FIND COMFORT IN YOUR NEW SHELL

*My appearance was who I thought I was. When that was taken away, the* real *me shined through. I was always there, but when I focused on my soul, I really came alive. Get quiet with yourself in a mirror and get comfortable with your new cover. Your beauty is from within and then from without.*

There is no way around it. Cancer changes a lot about your physical appearance, breast cancer especially. For a woman, it can feel like breast cancer steals away femininity. Breasts are, after all, a part of the female landscape that are a mark of womanhood. When they are taken away, it isn't easy. And breasts are only a part of the changes. There is also hair loss, which includes eyebrows and eyelashes; the scars from all the surgeries; the way your skin changes from all the chemo. It can truly be overwhelming if you don't go about it a certain way.

In the beginning of my journey, I hadn't a clue how I was supposed to handle so much at once. I didn't see that there was anything positive about what I was going through. All I could see was that I was being destroyed little by little. Mirrors became my worst enemies, and I began to feel like a foreigner in my own body, which I hardly recognized anymore.

My first major loss to breast cancer, in terms of my physical appearance, was the loss of my breasts. I've already touched upon some of the feelings I had about this, about how when I heard Beth might have to have a mastectomy and I told my doctor I didn't think I could lose *my* breasts, and how, as small as I was, the little bit I had meant a lot to me, but there is more to it than that—a lot more.

The morning that I went in to have my double mastectomy was a strange morning, as can be expected. I packed my little bag, and while I was packing, I threw a couple of bras in, along with jogging pants and a comfy T-shirt. After I tossed the bras in, I just stood there and stared down into my bag. It was then that reality hit me.

*Why am I packing bras?* I thought. And like that, the full force of everything that was happening came crashing down on top of me. Who knew something from Victoria's Secret could have such an effect?

I knew that I would have reconstruction and that it would start immediately, but still it would take time, and for that time, I wouldn't have breasts at all. It was something I never thought about, what you do without breasts, and suddenly I had to. So I took the bras back out and put them in a drawer, and then I did my best not to think about it anymore.

I couldn't eat anything that morning because of my surgery, so I had more time than I wanted to sit and consider what was happening. Luckily Duane is pretty quick about getting around, so I didn't have to sit too long, hungry and thinking about how later on that day there would be only rib cage and flesh where my breasts once were. I would glance down from time to time to see them and then try to shake the thought from my head. *They'll be back*, I assured myself.

We got to the hospital at around eight in the morning. I remember I was calm. It seemed like I had no emotions, really. I saw everybody around me; almost all my family was there, my mother-in-law, my children, my husband, and my siblings. Instead of being afraid, I thought, *This is beautiful. What a way to bring the family together.*

They were all getting along, happy and cheery, or that's what they showed me anyway. Duane was antsy though, and I knew he was scared of losing me, but I felt confident I would be okay, and I told him that.

The surgery went well, and when I came to, I was in a state of shock. I suppose that is the best way to describe it. I heard the doctor saying it went fine, and I knew Duane was in the room. As soon as I got my wits about me and remembered what was going on, I grasped my chest. It was tight with bandages.

I thought, *Oh my gosh, they're gone.* I could feel my ribs. It was like I thought it was just a dream, but when I felt my ribcage beneath the layers of gauze, hard and flat, I realized it wasn't a dream at all. Actually, it was kind of a nightmare. Have you ever had that recurring dream where all your teeth start to fall out? Do you know how panicked you feel during that dream? That was my reality as my hands groped along my new body.

I went through the same emotions you go through when you experience a death. It was like losing my dad again, and I just wanted to go to sleep. I didn't want to deal with anybody; I didn't want to talk to anybody. Let me just lay here and shut the door, turn off the lights, and leave me alone.

While I was trying to wrap my mind around all this, a nurse took a bra out of my bag, the one I had worn in, and said, "Oh, this is a cute bra."

"You can have it," I told her. "It will never fit me again. Go ahead and take it."

People started filling the room at that point. Mary came in, and the nurse said, "You must be a special person."

"Yeah, I am special all right," I said to her. "I'm the chosen one."

I didn't know what she was talking about as she said, "You have dozens of roses in a rainbow of colors, look up there," and then I looked up. She was referring to these huge vases filled with roses that just kept coming in. I hadn't even noticed them. There were two dozen roses in each vase up on a shelf. There were red ones, white ones, green ones, orange ones, pink ones; there were seven different choices of roses, twenty-four in a bouquet, just lining my hospital room wall. It was like the most beautiful rose garden ever had bloomed right there on the pale gray hospital room wall.

"Oh my gosh, they're gorgeous," I said.

My mom used to pray a novena of St. Theresa; to her a rose was always an answer to a prayer. I thought, *Wow, if a rose is an answer to your prayer, then all my prayers are answered because there are probably two hundred flowers sitting up there on the shelf.*

I was groggy for the rest of the day, but the next day when I was feeling a little better, they released me because of the H1N1 outbreak. I would be starting chemo soon, so we couldn't afford exposure to the flu in the meantime.

---

The weeks following my mastectomy were certainly not easy. In fact, they were a lot like torture from time to time. I would work through different emotions; sometimes I was in mourning, sometimes I was angry, and sometimes I felt sheer panic as I would remove my clothes to take a sponge bath or roll over on my chest in the night and realize that something was very different about my body. Every time I put on a blouse I wore pre-mastectomy I was reminded of what I had lost.

And then there was how I felt as a wife. This new body of mine didn't just affect me; it affected my husband, too, or so I thought. I felt awful because he was also being robbed of something. One night I had a breakdown in the heat of a passionate moment with my husband. I felt like I wasn't enough for him.

"Do you miss them?" I asked as I held back my tears.

"If I wanted to have them, I would go to California and see them." He smiled as he pulled me close to his chest. They were frozen in a lab in California for future research.

"Are you sure?" I asked again.

"Honey, all I care about is having you," he reassured me. "I'm just happy I have my Jeanne here. We will deal with the rest as it comes."

I was glad I talked to Duane about it. Hearing him joke and tell me it was okay helped ease some of the anxiety, but still I missed the sensation of my breasts. They made me feel like a woman. Duane said we could share his. He knows just what to say sometimes to take the edge off things. We both chuckled a little at that.

Talking about it really helped me get out of myself. I still harbored an awkward feeling as a woman, as a lover—like I wasn't giving my husband the whole package that he deserved, but I tried to keep in mind what he told me and to remember I'd have breasts again, some day.

As I waited for reconstruction, I tried to redirect my attention to the positive things about everything I was going through, like my breasts were taken from me, but I was so grateful to have working legs. I love to dance, and having no legs would be a greater devastation to me, so there really was a lot worse that could happen.

There's this term, *synecdoche, that's used for poetry mostly, but what it means is to take a part of something and make it the whole. I had done that with my breasts at first, but I had to see that there was more to me, a lot more, and that was liberating. But then I had to face everything again with chemo.*

The minute I was diagnosed with cancer, I just wanted to curl up and stay hidden from the world. I felt like I had a flashing neon sign on me that blinked "Cancer" and that everyone around me looked at me differently because of it. The last thing I wanted was to be looked at as a different person in the wake of all this, so it was hard for me to go out into public afterward. The double mastectomy and chemotherapy only made that neon sign seem brighter.

I started my chemo treatment, and during one of my doctor visits, my regular doctor had a fill-in who caught me off guard.

"How far out are you?" she asked, referring to my chemo.

"This is my first," I told her.

"Oh, well in the next fourteen days you will start losing your hair," she said without warning or any emotion tied to her words.

"Okay," I replied, a little shocked that she was so blunt about something so sensitive.

I found her words to be a little cruel. I thought, *How dare you say that to me?* Looking back I see she was only trying to keep me from complete shock, but in the moment I was agitated by what I saw as blatant insolence. I tried to get past my initial anger and move on to acceptance, so I went wig shopping with Kira.

"How about this one, Mom?" she'd ask, holding up a sassy, little blonde number.

"I don't know, Kira," I said. "I just don't think wigs are for me."

"Come on! It could be fun. New hair every day," Kira said, trying to pull something positive out of all this.

"Mommy wore wigs." I sighed as I ran my fingers through the auburn synthetic hair I was holding. "I just don't think it's my thing."

My doctor was right on. My head had been hurting so badly that even laying on a pillow was uncomfortable. By day twelve my hair started coming out in clumps, most of it in the areas that had been hurting the most. Apparently chemo makes your hair follicles dilate, thus the pain and then the loss of hair. I didn't care what was causing it though. I was devastated.

I had no idea how much hair I had until it all started falling out. I was mortified; I felt ashamed and vulnerable every time I saw wads of my own hair laying everywhere. It was all over the house; it came out while I was cooking and got in our food. Every morning I woke up and checked my pillow, and there it was, reminding me of the inevitable. Every time it happened I cried. I even started to wear hats to bed to try to slow the process down or at least to avoid having to see wads of hair first thing every morning when I woke up.

The shower always made it worse too because the hot water dilated the follicles more. I would step out of the shower, and as I combed my hair, more and more would come out. I'd feel panicked and nauseated as I watched in the mirror, combing out chunks of hair. *This isn't happening to me*, I thought.

When that started, I opted to clip my hair up, and I would not brush it after my shower, hoping to slow the process down. I was not ready for this loss. I was not ready to be that obvious, bald cancer patient. It wasn't just the hair, either. Of course, that was a big part since your hair is so much a part of your appearance, but it also was forcing me to accept the gravity of what was going on, and I didn't know if I wanted to do that yet. It was like staring death in the face every time I saw clumps of hair. It kind of was a death, the death of the Jeanne I once knew.

At one point I wondered who was shedding more, the dog or me. I knew that time was coming that I would just have to shave it all off, but I was a little hesitant at first, and a little angry, too.

Two weeks to the date after the doctor had warned me about my hair, I was in the bathroom getting ready to take a shower and it happened. As I was standing in my robe at the bathroom mirror, I started to brush my hair, which I swore I wasn't going to do. Clumps of hair came down with every stroke. I saw what was happening, and I would grab the hair and place it on the counter and then run the brush through again, more hair. Finally I put the brush down on the counter and began to mourn another loss. I stood there, my hair piled before me, and wept.

Kira was there in my bedroom talking to me through the door the whole time. She thought I was just getting ready to get in the shower though. She had no idea what was going on just on the other side of the door.

"Kira," I cried, "come in here now please."

"What's the matter, Mom?"

"You just need to come in here, please."

"Mom, what's the matter?" Kira asked again, but she never came in the bathroom. I think she was scared to go in there. Kira slowly opened the bathroom door and saw me with a handful of hair. I was weeping as I asked her, "Can you call your girlfriend that cuts hair and ask her to come out here to cut my hair at our house? And let's have a party." I was clutching a large amount of my hair in my hands.

"What?"

"I'm shaving my head," I said firmly. "Can you please set that up for me?"

"Okay," Kira said. It was almost a question more than a statement.

"Make sure Dad and Brad are home," I told her. "I don't want a whole lot of people here. I just want our immediate family."

So we set up the hair-cutting party. Kira's friend came in to do the cutting and shaving and so did the rest of the family. We had everyone over to take part in the shaving of my head. I wanted to start sharing my moments with those I loved, so I wanted everyone to be there. Some of my sisters brought wine for the occasion.

"Oh, I should not drink," I said as glasses were being passed around.

"You can have a little," Mary said and handed me a glass.

"I'm saving mine for the big event," I said with a nervous little smile.

*Supportive kiss mid-haircut*

And so it began. Everyone was telling funny stories to try to lighten the mood, which helped, but there were also a few tears shed for the occasion. Each time another cut was made, I would feel my hair and let it sink in and then brace myself for the next chop.

Eventually the razor came out, and slowly I watched all my hair fall from my scalp. It felt like I was undressing in front of the entire room. Suddenly my brother Mike spoke up.

"I'll be next," he said. "You won't be the only bald one this way, sis."

And so Mike got his head shaved too in the chair next to mine. What was the biggest shock though was seeing Brad walk out of the bathroom with his head shaved as well. He had decided he was going to shave his head with me too to show his support. I lost hair that day, but I gained a lot too.

*Me with my bald supporters: Brad and Mike*

When it was all over, everyone told me how great I looked, but I couldn't bring myself to believe them as I looked into the mirror and saw this strange bald woman staring back. I certainly wasn't me now, and it was even more outwardly apparent than it had been with the mastectomies. This everyone could see, and a padded bra wouldn't help.

I ended up losing all my eyelashes as well the day after my twenty-eighth radiation treatment. It was a final blow, but also a revelation. It started just like the hair had, with the painful sensation. Then I'd see eye-lashes coming out in little bundles. I thought, *Not my eyelashes. Take my hair, God, but not my eyelashes.* They seemed to be the one thing I had left, but they went too.

It took about two weeks of shock, self-pity, and constant vulnerability for me to decide this was not my fault. I decided to embrace it whole heartedly and to do this elegantly and stand tall. Cancer may have been taking my body for the time, but I would not let it take my soul. With that thought in mind, I started to reevaluate how I looked at every loss I'd had to deal with since my diagnosis.

As I worked to change my outlook, I realized that my looks meant everything to me. I had spent my life hiding behind my makeup and hair, and I was strug-gling to let go of that. So one day I sat and sobbed, *Why me, God?* But as I was looking in the mirror, I thought, *Why not me?* And a calm came over me.

For the first time I caught a glance of my naked eyes in the mirror, and I stared at them for about half an hour. I saw beauty, and it was coming from my soul. I thought, *I will do this with grace and ease and be a teacher for those like me. It is not our fault. You are beautiful as you always have been. Show the world the inner beauty that has always been there.*

Going to work was hard in the beginning, facing people without my hair, breasts, and eyelashes. At first I noticed lots of whispers and people sneaking peeks as I passed, trying to see me without me noticing. I even saw a doctor's jaw drop as he craned his head to get a look. I had to give myself constant pep talks, and I guess those pep talks started to pay off because I started to notice a different kind of attention once I walked with my head held high.

While the first few days felt like torture for me, things eventually started to get better. One day I was working beside a doctor and he stopped and looked right at me.

"Jeanne, you have the most beautiful eyes," he said. "If the hospital had a contest, you would definitely win."

"Thank you," I told him. "You're so kind. But it is not the eyes. It's the windows to my soul."

I began to let my experiences empower me. *They are looking at your inner beauty*, I would tell myself. And instead of hiding my diagnosis, I decided that I'd share my story with as many people as I could, because you never know if or when their lives may be affected by cancer.

I let people know I am Jeanne, I have cancer, and I am here to talk. I let people ask questions, and I gave them honest answers. I also made jokes at times but wasn't afraid to cry either.

I found that I did have some control yet, because I was still me and I didn't have to let cancer take that from me. If I just kept telling people about my journey, it could become just a story.

So I say now, cut your hair shorter at the first sign of hair loss; it's easier to tolerate and less noticeable on floors. Don't be afraid of the physical changes; just embrace them because you are not your breasts or your hair or your eyelashes. You are an essence much bigger than all that, and no disease will ever touch that part of you. Let my experience help take you to the next level.

My mind-set shift changed everything for me, and suddenly I was not focusing on what I had lost but on what I had gained. It was then I started to find my happiness again. I couldn't be happy when I made myself look at my body or caught glimpses of it as I stepped into the shower, but then something happened. I began to see my blessings.

The real truth about happiness is when you look in the mirror and see yourself exactly as you are and you realize that no matter what you see, the real you is still in there, then you have reached something huge. My biggest challenge turned out to be my greatest blessing because I began to look past the exterior and really focus on the interior. I began to realize that, one, I wasn't defined solely by my physical self, and two, I still had a lot left physically anyway.

*Before and After chemo*

When I began to change so much on the outside, who I really was came out, and I felt like I didn't have to protect my inner self anymore. All those years of growing up I didn't want to get hurt, so I protected that little person inside, but now all of a sudden that little person inside was what I had left, and she was protecting me. I felt good about that. I feel so energized and energetic because of it. I thought, *Okay, I can do this*. All of a sudden everything I was just totally did a flip on me, and I was finally able to be Jeanne, the real Jeanne.

## MY DIAGNOSIS FROM ANOTHER POINT OF VIEW

I wasn't the only one who experienced my changing physical appearance; so did everyone around me—specifically my family. For a family member, it can be taxing to watch someone you've known and loved your whole life transform in front of you. I have been telling Kira's side throughout the book, but this time I'm going to use Kira's own words to describe her side of this transformation (my hair loss in particular). The following is how Kira experienced one of my major changes:

> Today was one of those days that you know is bound to happen, but you hope in your whole heart that you can sneak past it, the "who is going to shave my head" conversation. I never really understood until today what really happens with chemo patients and why they lose their hair. Apparently the chemotherapy dilates

the hair follicles, which is why the hair pretty much just falls out. Learn something new every day I guess; not really a lesson that I expected to learn in my lifetime.

Anyway, after a series of emotional conversations here and there, we decided that it would be a little too traumatic for one of us to do it, so a friend of mine is going to be coming over to my parents' house to do it. Mom wants to make sure that whoever does it makes the situation as light as possible, so of course when it does happen she will have a series of what I'm calling the "chemo mohawks."

Mom had said that her scalp hurt (Dad told me that that was the beginning of the follicles dilating). She was nauseous this morning, but that seemed to come and go throughout the day. So far the smell of food seems to make it worse. She was making pancakes this morning with Kitana and got a little concerned with a few hairs falling out. It may be just normal, something that would happen anyway, but a person waiting for "it" to happen notices each strand as it falls, I think.

It's going to be really hard to watch her go through this. I've offered to shave my head right along with her, but she said this morning that she doesn't want to look at us with the bald heads as well and be reminded constantly. I can understand what she means, but I just don't want her to have to go through this herself.

We had one of those tough days. Mom is completely worn out after another sleepless night, one hour of sleep. And to top off that stress, I decided to push her into the wig ordering today. I figured at least if we get them ordered, she may have some options already here for her when the time comes. I ordered her six wigs, all a little different. I think it will be kind of fun to see which wigs she chooses for her mood for each different day.

She's not handling her hair falling out as well as I think she hoped she would. She just says, "It's devastating," and I know if any of us were sitting in her situation, we would think the same thing. But I just want to take a second to say to her here that it's not her hair that got her where she is. When people talk about others, it's generally not about their looks; it's about their genuine personality, their character, and their kind and caring hearts. And anyone who knows my mom knows that she is overflowing with those. Don't lose sight of who you are. Don't let your hair define you because you have *so* much more going for you. Your hair will grow back.

Tuesday morning I got to my parents' house, and Mom was in the bathroom getting ready. I sat while she brushed her hair and cried, clearing out the brush and piling the hair strands on the countertop so she could take another swipe. Each time there were just as many strands as the last, and it seemed never-ending. I teared up. It's really hard to watch her have to go through this!

We knew it was going to happen, and no matter how much you try to prepare yourself for it, there is still the shock. Mom says that she's looking in the mirror, watching it, but she can't help but think that its not happening and feeling like she's pulling out someone else's hair. She tries really hard to keep a happy face on, but you know inside that she's scared.

The Day:

Saturday everyone gathered at my parents' around 7:00 p.m. to be there to support Mom. Everyone had a few drinks—Mom was saving her glass (she could only have one) for the cut.

I thought it all went pretty well, a few tears here and there, but ultimately everyone tried to make it the least traumatic as possible. I think everyone knew that they were there to try and make it less devastating. So the jokes and stories continued, except each time Mom reached up to feel how short each step was, there was a pause of silence; I think to give her a moment to react.

After Mom was done, her brother Mike decided that in support he was next in the chair. He shaved his head as well, and while that was happening, my brother called me into the bathroom to secretly shave his head to support the cause (he wanted to surprise Mom.... and surprised she was)!

I think it all went pretty well. Mom looks as beautiful as she did before the cut. She doesn't believe anyone when they tell her that. We all kind of knew it was going to be a little bit of a process for her to accept and embrace her new self. She says when she looks into the mirror, she expects to see herself, but now there seems to always be someone else peering back at her. She said she feels like her whole body is now foreign to her. But she really does look great.

I guess that others could see from the get go what took me a little time to see myself. Kira certainly did. And once I got used to it and was receptive to it, others stopped gawking and started simply asking questions, which I much preferred to being silently stared at from around corners as I passed, like I was a leper or something from another planet.

One day three girls in my department were very inquisitive and curious about my breasts and my hair. They wanted to see my bald beauty, so I drew them a picture of my chest and exposed my bald head to them. I was very comfortable, and that was totally unlike anything I would ever do, but I wanted to let people know that this is a big deal for many of the sufferers of breast cancer, both the patients and loved ones, or any other cancer really. The whole process hurts many people.

You become vulnerable and then get tired of the process and then get strong. The thing to remember is it is not your fault. You did not do this. Stand tall and talk about it. It not only helps you, but your openness may also help a few people along the way.

So don't let the changes keep you in hiding; be bold and let the real you shine through. This is your chance. Let the curse of cancer be a blessing in disguise, and use it for yourself and for others. I felt stripped of who

I was in the beginning, but really I was stripped of my façade and left with this amazing inner beauty, the genuine me.

# LESSON 8:

# SEXY IS A
# STATE OF MIND

*Have fun with your new look. Try on different clothes, and get comfortable in your new body. Being sexy comes from within and how you feel about yourself as you are. Think of yourself as sexy, and that is what you will become.*

I always thought my looks were me. I always had makeup on, and my hair was always done. I never went out of the house any other way. Once I started all my treatments and had one thing after the next taken away though, I was suddenly dealing this vulnerability that I had never felt before in my life.

After my head-shaving party, I'd look at myself and think, *Oh my gosh, this is how bald people feel*. Some are really proud of their baldness, but I wasn't feeling so at home with it in the beginning. To me it felt like standing naked in front of everyone and exposing everything. Being bald was a whole new sense of who I am not.

*Duane shaving my random hair spikes*

I was embarrassed of my head and all I could think was, *What am I gonna do now?*

At the head-shaving party, my brother Mike, the one who always put on Mom's pink lipstick, made the comment, "You always have to do your hair. Now you don't have to!" He was just trying to lighten the mood.

"Oh yeah, look," I said, pointing to my head, and I started crying. "They took my breasts away from me, and now they're taking my hair. That is not funny."

"Jeanne, you're beautiful now that you really have to bring out who you are," my brother, who was never serious or emotional, said to me.

"I don't want to be hurt," I said with tears rolling down my face. "I don't want people to trample on who I really am. I'm scared."

I thought about what Mike said, and for the next two weeks, I'd go in the mirror and I'd look at who I am, and if people came over, I'd quickly put a hat on. I'd hide it and try wigs on. My mom wore a wig a lot, and I thought that maybe I could pull it off too, even if I was hesitant at first. Kira had done a great job and helped me pick out a few cute ones. Her wedding was coming up, so I wanted something cute to wear for that. When I tried putting them on though, I'd put them on backward, or crooked sometimes. Kira would straighten them up for me, but they just didn't work.

I was a little put off by the wig experience, but I wasn't going to admit defeat. The words *grace* and *ease* came back to me, and I convinced myself that I could do this with elegance, just like I did everything else to that point once I accepted it. So I started getting scarves and really nice hats and wearing those out. Once I got comfortable with those, I thought, *Whoa, this is really nice.* I was cold all the time, so I got a hat to keep me warm. I began to see myself with my scarves as looking pretty darn good. I started matching my scarves to my outfit.

Then I went to class with my sister Kelly to a class where they teach you how to do your makeup working around all the aftermath of chemo. We had fun applying lipstick and blush.

"Jeanne, you're the only bald one in this class," Kelly leaned over and whispered.

"Oh, thanks for that little reminder," I said back to her.

"No, Jeanne, I'm pushing you out of your comfort zone," she said. "They need a mannequin to help put the scarves on. You're the only bald one in this class. The people are not gonna know what it looks like unless they put it in a bald person."

"Kelly, I couldn't get in front all of these women," I scoffed. "You go up there, take your clothes off, and see how you like it."

"Jeanne, you can do this."

"Okay, okay. I'll do it, but only for these women so they know they can do it with grace," I finally agreed.

Every day I would push through my comfort zone with grace and ease. There were a lot of times I'd fail; I'd just lie back and feel pathetic and pity myself. That day I wasn't doing to do that. So I got up in the chair and said, "Okay, I'm your mannequin."

"Really?" the instructor asked.

"Really," I said.

"Good."

I took my hat partially off and kind of held on to it for a little bit. I started second guessing my courage once the hat was off.

"I'm not sure if I'm ready for this," I finally said.

"You'll be fine," the instructor assured me as she took off my hat and spun me around for everybody to see. I got so many compliments in my class. I thought, *Wow, this really feels good.*

The instructor used me, putting hats and different wigs and scarves and stuff on my head, and we learned a lot together. How to put mascara on without eyelashes, how to put makeup on after the chemo has destroyed your skin—it's really thin and soft, and so there's a technique to applying things like eyeliner and whatnot.

We also learned how to master colors and what creams to put on. But mostly I learned that bald is beautiful, and I would carry that around with me, so much so that I was even ready for photos to showcase it.

As I got comfortable with my new look, I learned to really own it. I even decided to have professional bald photos done. I had a choice to stand up for other women, and I would not sit down. I chose to show how life could go on after cancer. I would embrace this new part and use it as a tool to keep fighting. There was no reason for me to hide who I was, and I thought photos were a perfect way to prove that. So I did a photo shoot with my new bald head, and I held that bald head high. I may have looked different, but my brother was right. I was as beautiful as ever. Maybe even more so because I appreciated life like I never had before, and I think that came through.

My head wasn't the only thing changing about me. I was also on my way to another transformation, but this one would be giving me something back: my breasts. During all this I was doing the expansions, which were little bag-type things put in my chest to prepare for reconstruction. For me that was the fun part. It was a reminder that I was going to have breasts again. Two or three days a week I would go back to the plastic surgeon, and she would add a little bit of fluid to my expanders. Every day I went I knew was a step close to having a feminine body again.

The day of the long-awaited surgery finally arrived, and I went in with Duane at half past six.

"This is the day," I said with a smile. "I'm going to look like a woman again."

"Jeanne, you've always looked like a woman," Duane said as he grabbed my hand. "A beautiful one at that. You don't need boobs for that."

"I love you," I said as I squeezed his hand. "But it will be nice to have them, don't you think?" I said with a little chuckle.

"I won't complain," he said.

My surgery was scheduled for 8:00 a.m. My plastic surgeon came in and did some markings on my breasts, and at noon my nurse pulled out my IV and told me I could go home when I felt ready. I got dressed right away (I like to be sick in my own home, if I'm going to be sick).

My sister Kelly texted me, "How are you doing? Love you!"

"My 'DDs' have been placed. I am dizzy, sore, and groggy. But my breasts are so large they pull the wrinkles out of my neck. Two for one special at the surgical suite," I sent back as I giggled and fell back to sleep in the recliner.

When the swelling had finally gone down some, I got my first peek at my new breasts, and the plastic surgeon really did an awesome job. Once I could take the bandages off, I put a bra on for the first time in a year. Not the sexy kind, a surgical bra. But it was a step closer to the real thing, and I was glad to do it. I never thought I'd miss bras.

Time went by, and I began to feel a little more like myself every day. There were scars, and I still didn't have the hair I once did, but I was starting to see that sexy is not just what you look like; it's a state of mind. It was as much about confidence as it was my physical appearance, and the more confident I got, the sexier I became.

I was making real strides in loving the new me, but I won't say that it wasn't constant work to maintain grace through it all. I pushed myself constantly though and refused to succumb to the negativity that would sneak up on me every once in a while. As my hair came back, I could tell it wasn't going to be the same, but I would just say to myself, *You can make this work*, and go on.

I even started to feel at ease at work around coworkers and strangers. For the first time, I felt like I didn't have to have hair or eyelashes. I still had stares occasionally. I had people looking at me because I had to match my hat with my uniform. Women did most of the peeking at me from the corner of their eyes, but I took it all with grace because I knew who I was and what I was: beautiful inside and out. The guys would come up to me and say, "Oh my gosh! Is that Jeanne?"

"It is indeed," I'd tell them.

"Oh, I could recognize those eyes anywhere," some would say. The windows to my soul.

The guys were very open, and they would ask questions.

"What happened?"

"So how are you doing?"

Women were more reluctant for some reason, but I let that empower me, too. *They're thinking I'm pretty hot right now*, I'd tell myself when I saw a "peeker." I just giggled inside. *Oh, they're wishing they were me.* I was getting this great body out of something I used to hide because people teased me about it, and I was looking pretty hot, thanks to my plastic surgeon.

---

Then came Kira's wedding. It was the first time I'd really dressed up since cancer came into our lives two years before. I wore a beautiful black dress and black headgear.

*Preparing for Kira's wedding*

My surgeon did a great job. I looked like a piece of art, well put together, and I wore it proudly. Lots of heads turned, and I made up a story that empowered me.

Kira had tried to convince me to leave my scarf off the day of her wedding.

"You have hair now, Mom," she told me. "You don't need it."

"I just don't feel ready yet, Kira," I explained. "I want all eyes on you. It's your day. I don't want people coming up to you and talking about my hair."

"Okay, but I think you should leave if off," Kira said, finally giving in. I thought she was finished with that, but I was wrong.

Kira and I decided we would do a mother-daughter dance at her wedding. We had been through a lot in the last year, so we wanted to do something special at such a momentous time for all of us. We danced to Edwin McCain's "I'll Be," and as I listened to the lyrics, I looked at the amazing woman that I had raised. I really was the greatest fan of her life, and she mine. As the song ended, I wrapped my arms around Kira, and then something huge happened. She pulled my scarf off and kissed my cheek.

I stood there in the middle of the dance floor without my scarf, and for a moment I panicked. Tears came to my eyes, and I thought I might pass out from anxiety. But then I looked around, and I saw the tears in everyone's eyes, tears because they loved me and supported me. I was absolutely moved by the entire thing, and I was glad that Kira had done it. It was just more proof to me that I didn't have to hide a thing.

## MY DIAGNOSIS FROM ANOTHER PERSPECTIVE

Now that we are nearing the end of the book, I will lean more on Kira's words to describe her experiences. I know that, like me, Kira was moving through different emotional phases dealing with my cancer. Although I was the one experiencing the physical changes, she was there by my side the entire time cheering me on. I said Kira is the strong one, and the way she pulled me through my insecurities with my looks was no exception to that rule. The following are some of the ways Kira felt while I was coming to terms with my new self and the way she saw it:

> I think that Mom's fear that she *looked* different was the reason it was so hard returning to work and everything was such a big deal—because people were starting to accept her the way she was with this disease and all of a sudden she's crawling back to another side.
>
> I knew she had a tough time with all of it, so it was always good to see her having really good days. The day she did the photo shoot was one of those. I was happy to see that it seemed as though she was having fun with it.
>
> I stopped over there at eleven in the morning, and she seemed pretty excited to do a few family photos. I think the last one we had taken I was probably about twelve years old, so it's been a while. Mom was freezing before we even

stepped foot outside, but you could tell that she really wanted the photos.

She was also pretty excited about the new scarves and hats that she'd been getting in the mail from a few different cancer foundations. She tried to make the best out of this experience, and trying out new things different from what she would go with normally lifted her spirits. I think she is really starting to embrace her newfound beauty! And it was great to see her enjoying it!

Although I loved the fun my mom was having with her scarves, I thought it was time for her to let them go, so I made sure that would happen, at my wedding! And now the scarves are put away. I pulled it off during a dance at my wedding. She wasn't quite ready for it yet, but she'd been saying that they were going to get put away the day after anyway, so I just figured what a better way to do the unveiling then on a day filled with love.

It was just instant tears from both of us. It was a pretty emotional time. It's one of those things that you have to be there to experience. She was without hair for six or seven months. That was a pretty big event, and I was glad to be the one to help her do it.

---

With cancer, everything comes in stages. It is almost like you are an infant, learning to live life all over again. It can be tough at first, but we have more control than we may think. Our control comes from our ability to adjust our outlook.

In the beginning of the process, with the mastectomies and then the hair loss, I felt helpless and defeated. Once I got tired of the self-pity, though, I turned things on their heads. I decided that I could either mourn the loss of the old me forever or get to know and love the new me—the new me physically, as I had found that some parts of you never go away. Once I started to see the bright side, things changed a lot for me.

I may have lost some, but I was slowly gaining a lot back. My hair was finally coming back, a little differently, and I had brand-new breasts. I remember the first time I put on my swimsuit after the surgery. I looked at myself and commended my plastic surgeon and my general surgeon. They did an awesome job, even though the process was not complete.

So I didn't have to feel robbed of my identity, my femininity, or my beauty. I just had to get to know myself in a new way and appreciate all I had, and that is just what I did. I opted to see the rainbow instead of focusing on the storm.

# LESSON 9:

# STAYING STRONG AND FINDING YOURSELF ONCE AGAIN

*Rebuild your broken body. Become strong physically and mentally. Feed your soul positive information, and exercise your body to keep you emotionally, mentally, and physically resilient.*

I remember after my hair loss, going back to work was such a hurdle for me to overcome. It had been twelve weeks since I had seen anyone, and there I was with no hair and no breasts. I felt like I was walking in nude. As time passed, however, I started to embrace the new me and see the beauty that was really there. And just when I was getting comfortable in my skin again, I faced yet another crossing: revealing my hair and my new body.

When I look back at everything, it all seems to have flown by, despite all the heart-wrenching obstacles. When I think of everything that has happened since that first spot showed up at the chiropractor's office, I feel like it all happened to someone else, like it was an outer body experience that left an emotional scar, but I'm doing all I can to see those scars as medals of honor for making it through one battle after the next. *You've got nothing to be ashamed of,* I tell myself. *You're still standing with your head held high. You're going on for yourself and for others.*

Although I'm finding myself once again, post-chemo, post-surgery, post-completely different life, I still feel fear bubble up inside me sometimes when I walk past the mirror after getting out of the shower. I'm afraid to look at myself—afraid I won't recognize what I see. I also didn't like looking at my body because all I could see was the cancer that destroyed my being, emotionally and physically.

My body was a constant reminder every day that I inflicted horrible pain on my family whom I always protected. I had to change my mind-set, though, and instead of seeing a ravaged body, I had to start to see a body that was ready to be healthy again—a body, and a me, that deserved to be built back up. I had to see myself in a new light, and so I began to do that.

After spending so much time with scar tissue and bandages where my breasts once were, even after reconstruction it was easy to let myself slip into a mini-panic attack when I was naked and a mirror was nearby. When these anxieties took hold of me, I learned to sit and breathe and meditate for a bit. When I stopped to do this, I would become calm and realize that my breasts were beginning to feel real, like a part of me. I realized that my life was not over as I knew it but coming to new chapters. I just needed to be still and recognize that fact.

I feel so alive when I am able to meditate, quiet my mind, and bring myself to a place where I can think, pray, and beg God for my future goodness. The quiet helps me concentrate, be happy, and process the tough things in life. It also prepares me for growth and allows me time to see how much of it I have made in the last couple of years. Slowly, with the help of God, prayer, meditation, my family, and the amazing support system around me, I'm seeing myself as whole again, but all this comes in stages that must be worked through.

Another part of rediscovering me was getting used to my new hair. I had thought the hard part was losing my hair, but I found out that growing it back wasn't exactly easy either. It was devastating for me. My hair looked so different, its texture and color, and besides that, I had this boyish hair coming in until it got short and sassy. Even when it reached that stage though, I was reluctant to remove my hat. I spent so long wearing scarves and hats that they became a kind of security blanket for me.

Kira helped me step outside my comfort zone when she pulled my scarf off at her wedding. I didn't think I was ready or strong enough, but she showed me I was. Kitana also played a role in helping me come to terms with the new me.

"Grandma, you don't need that hat," she told me as I walked her to school one day. "You have lots of pretty hair now," she said as she pulled my hat off. From the mouths of babes, as they say.

My first day back to work after Kira's wedding, *hat-less*, I had a beautiful head of hair, half an inch long and curly. I was nervous to go back to work, and very cold with no hat on, but it was time, and I knew it. As strange as it may sound, walking in without a hat felt a lot like my first day back as a bald woman. There were all the questions and the silent stares. I was vulnerable all over again.

*Playtime on a "good" day*

"Do you perm your hair?" one woman asked. I have less than a half inch of hair, so my hair couldn't even wrap a curler.

"No, I paid for perms all my life, but this one really cost me a lot," I told her. "It's natural from chemo."

Another girl asked me one day, "What are you doing with your hair? It's extra curly today."

"My husband and I sat together all night and placed pin curls in it," I told her with a straight face. "It gave us a ton of quality time because it took *forever*."

I learned to take the questions lightly and have fun with them instead of feeling threatened by them or letting cancer win. I made up funny responses that made me chuckle a little instead of hurt.

There were times I'd forget that my hair was so short. I'd forget for a moment and think that I still had long hair, but then I'd snap back to reality. In the beginning, there was a kind of sadness I felt when I'd realize that I'd never have the same hair again, but I decided at a point that I was finished mourning my loss, and it was time to start living again and loving everything about the person I had become—scars, new breasts, different hair and all.

Once I got comfortable and my outlook started to shift, I changed my hair, short brown-black hair with reddish orange highlights. I wouldn't be held down by any of the past hurts or losses anymore. I would take the best from everything that had happened and use it to empower me. I had been focused on my losses, but I would refocus to new growth. I saw my life as taking new paths, especially once my incisions healed. I began to embrace the new me, my new body.

I can't say that there aren't always bumps and road-blocks when you're making such a triumphant comeback. Just a week or so after I was feeling really great about my new look, a seven-year-old girl and her mom walked by, and I heard the little girl asked, "Mom, is that a girl or a boy?"

I was thrown back a little by that. I wanted to break down and allow self-pity to take over. It took a lot to get comfortable with my new hair again mentally, and one thoughtless comment can put you back to a bad place quickly, but I knew that I couldn't let the comment take away the ground I had gained, so I gave myself a couple of minutes and regrouped. I got quiet, and then I got even stronger.

I found that, as a survivor, it helps tremendously to use upbeat words. When someone asks, "How are you doing?" I like to reply with, "Fantastic!" Getting into the right crowd is vital too, with folks who appreciate what they have. I want to surround myself with people who recognize every day is a gift. I also started to jot down my accomplishments, say hello to strangers, brighten my lipstick, and do my makeup. I needed to make a positive environment at all times, so I took, and still take, every step I can toward positivity, and I try to do it in all areas of my life.

In the beginning of all this, I simply saw my body being destroyed, and I felt that there was nothing I could do about it—that I had to sit and watch as everything crumbled. When I got my mind-set adjusted, I had this epiphany—I *do* still have control; I just have to take initiative and exercise it. I could eat different ways to nourish my body, practice positive thinking, go to spas, and do yoga to relieve the stress that the whole experience causes. I could also put together special gifts for the cancer sufferers who attend the clinics—positive CDs, recipes, detoxify soaps, oils, yoga tapes—to help in every life as their battle continues. I found what a difference replenishing your mind, body, and soul could make, so I pass that gift on to others, and that has helped me and them.

Another gift I gave myself and others was walking for cancer. I spent so much time sick and worn down, but getting myself to walk for miles again I knew was something that would help me to grow and to heal, mentally and physically. It would be grueling at times, I knew, but the end result would be worth it all.

I didn't walk for an eight-month stretch at one point because of a busy life of doctors, chemo, radiation, fatigue, anger, and pain, but finally I conquered a six-mile walk.

The physical pain of the walking removes you from the emotional pain you are in. The walking helped not only rebuild my body but also bring clarity. *You will survive the pain you are in; others have and you will too*, I began to realize as I worked through the pain.

Once I proved to myself that I could overcome the pain and I got my body going again, I set my goals even higher. Although I had neuropathy in my feet and was in agony at times, I pushed myself to keep going and trained for a *sixty-mile* cancer walk. The walk was held to raise money for research to assist in the cure and to help with treatment for those who couldn't afford it.

While I was training, I took seven pairs of shoes back to the store, looking for just one pair that would be comfortable. With the neuropathy in my toes and feet, there wasn't a shoe in the world that was going to help too much, but still I was determined to walk the whole sixty miles. It was my victory walk. For all those who couldn't participate, I stood and walked for them.

To prepare for the walk, I gathered about six heavy blankets and a hat. It was 74 degrees during the day, but I knew at night it would get down to 50 degrees at night, and I dreaded that. I wasn't going to let anything deter me from the walk, though. It would be a battle, just like cancer had been, but the thing is, we are all going to fight some kind of battle until the day we die, and the question is, are we going to win or lose? I choose to win all my battles, or try my hardest to win, and this was no exception.

So regardless of pain or exhaustion or cold, damp nights, I would go and fight the fight, and I will always be glad for that because I pushed my body to do its best again (and made it through all sixty miles!), but most importantly, I was able to meet other bold families fighting the same fight, and while some stories were sad ones of losing the good fight, there were also inspiring ones that fueled me. The inspiring ones I keep close to me—I pull in all the positivity I can from them.

*3 day cancer walk with my sisters: Kelly Mayers and Mary Posch*

## MY DIAGNOSIS FROM ANOTHER PERSPECTIVE

When you are battling cancer, you're not fighting the fight alone, and you're also not the only one being affected by everything that is going on. Although loved ones are there in the thick of it with you, they may see things a bit differently. The following are some thoughts and feelings that Kira had about my battle to rebuild and stay positive:

> When my mom is going through something
> that she doesn't want people to know that she

is afraid of, or that she is in pain and hurting, she tries to throw them off to another direction, and she uses positive vibes or she jokes about it. Like the time we were in the hospital after mom went through her mastectomy surgery, right when she woke up she cracked this joke: "Oh, now I don't have to go bra shopping anymore." I think she's looking for the things to make fun out of all this, trying to ease the tension for everybody else. For us, though, we felt like sometimes she was hiding behind it.

I know she's doing it for all of us though, joking and making light of things. She went through this training course that discussed chemo and cancer and all that, and I'm sure that it stressed the importance of being positive, so she does her best to do that no matter what. It can feel like we're being shielded from things sometimes, but I see what she's doing, and I know she's doing it to help all of us. Even if it does feel like a cover sometimes, though, I think it's important too, and I like to do things that help her keep that positive attitude.

During the chemo, I did a lot of researching online for cute little scarves and stuff. We went wig shopping, and after she ordered a ton of wigs. She decided that she didn't like them though, so she just went with the scarves. We just did little things to make her feel good about herself. It's really hard for me to see her in so much pain, so I wanted to do what I could to brighten her day. Luckily I have a secret weapon named Kitana that also helped out with that.

One day Mom and Kitana had a bake-a-thon. Mom measured all the ingredients and put them in the oven, and Kitana did the rest, the mixing and "testing." I think all grandmas like to sugar up their grandkids before they send them home, but I was okay with that because it seemed to bring Mom's spirits up a bit. Any time she's having a bad day, I can bring Kitana over to visit her, and she can always get Mom to crack a smile, so I spent a lot of time at her house because I wanted to be sure Mom was smiling.

Although I wish with all my heart that Mom would have never had to go through any of this, I do think it has brought me closer to her personally. I tried to go to Mom and Dad's and spend as much time with Mom as I could after her diagnosis. I also wanted to keep my kids around her as much as possible. She says it helped her get her mind off the things. We're more aware of her feelings, and that's a real accomplishment because Mom was really good about being quiet about her feelings before.

One problem about being so close to my mom, though, is that when you're so close, you don't think any fight is ever hard enough. I want her to do everything she can to make sure she is around here for my kids. I want my kids to be able to experience her like I have. I think that sometimes that makes me come off as pushy to Mom, but I just want to help fight with her. I guess if I step back and look at what she's done, I would see she is doing a pretty good job of fighting herself.

After radiation, Mom insisted she do a victory cancer walk, which was sixty miles in three miles (and the pedometer said seventy-one miles). She tried like eight pairs of shoes prior to the walk but ended up settling for a pair that didn't help her feet. She said they hurt from the first mile on. Her feet were swollen from neuropathy, but she still did the whole thing.

It rained the first day, the second day was good walking weather, and the third day was *hot*! The walk was hard, amazing, emotional, but a victory! She heard lots of stories she didn't want to hear, but she was also amazed to see all the survivors. It was exhausting for her, but she did raise her total goal this year thanks to all her supporters!

We were thankful for everyone that showed at the beginning and ending ceremonies; it was nice to see the support system all come together. Most of all, it was amazing to see how my mom was really able to push through everything, the pain and the weather and everything else. She proves to me all the time how strong she is.

———

After my battle, I have come to the conclusion that self-acceptance is the key to heal some of the rage and come to an understanding when you are fighting something so overwhelming. You don't have to live at an angry level. In fact, living there is only going to steal life and happiness away from you; it's letting the other side win. I have decided that I will never just let the other side win, not without a fight, and part of that fight is staying positive and working on my resilience.

I've had an amazing life, and to fixate only on the times that have been not so amazing only robs me of the joy that exists in the good parts. I plan on taking back control of my mental and physical well-being—it feels so good to accomplish something as little as going for a walk. I let my spirit tell my body what is going to happen.

For anyone fighting their own fight, the inner storm keeps pressing on, but you must find your inner strength and courage to overcome it. Take every step you can to become more positive in all that you do, because wrapping yourself in all the negative feelings, or even simply standing still and letting apathy take over, won't pull you through to the other side. A fight this big is worth fighting, so use all the tools you have to come out the victor.

# Epilogue:

# LOVE HELPS MEND ALL WOUNDS

*Surround yourself with loved ones. Write letters to clear your mind. You don't have to send the letters, but it can be very cleansing to free the words that you really mean to say. Don't be afraid to tell those in your life that you appreciate them. Most of us hold back and forget to acknowledge the good. Don't let giving gratitude be a regret for your future.*

Today I thank people in my life for just showing up. I am beyond generous with my thank-yous and my compliments. If I think someone is beautiful or looks great, I let them know that. Recognizing and verbalizing all that is good is how I stand up.

I stand up to cancer today. Cancer connects us all, but when we truly stand up to cancer, that is when we truly connect. This disease has two faces: hope and fear. I send gratitude to each and every plastic surgeon, general surgeon, oncologist, radiologist, general doctor, nurses, physical therapist, scheduler, therapist, specialist, family, friends, and their teams who have touched my life. If they had not been a part of my journey, I may have chosen fear instead of hope.

I refuse to hide my emotions anymore. I'm not afraid to cry, laugh, or be grateful for people who have touched my life. I offer nothing less than my own beating heart for anyone who helped me on this long, draining journey. With the help of my doctors, surgeons, family, friends, and support system, I was able to build a strong foundation, spiritually, physically, emotionally, and mentally, and with a stable foundation, we can pull through anything.

Now that I have made it through so much, my intension is to always live each day with *no* regrets—to give thanks and praise whenever I can and tell people exactly how I feel. I'm not afraid to express anything anymore. Life is too short. Because of that, I have these letters to share with those who really pulled me through.

## A LETTER TO
## MY PLASTIC SURGEON AND NURSE

To you both,

First off, how lucky was I to happen to fall upon the both of you. You are a great team; your personalities and expertise complement each other.

I was up several times last night thinking about the both of you. 1:00 a.m., 2:00 a.m., 3:00 a.m....crying, tears falling down, soaking my pillow, as if I'd lost something great. Oh, but I did.

I told my husband I have this deep and significant, overwhelming sense of my loss, my husband wanting to fix me but not knowing how. I feel compelled to write you both this note because that's what I do nowadays. I like people to know in my life how much they mean to me and not miss the opportunity to show my gratitude. I had not planned on writing this as early as 4:00 a.m., but you're worth it. So this morning I take steps to a sound mind and soul by writing you both an appreciation letter.

September 28, 2009, my journey began, with a different nurse and plastic surgeon. I kept this a secret from my family for a while in the beginning stages of biopsy and mammograms. I didn't want my father to know; he was my only parent left, and he was suffering from cancer, and so was my sister. I did not want to burden them with yet another nightmare or any more devastating news.

A year later my nightmare came alive again, cancer—the monster was back in my family. What do you want? "God," I pleaded, "please use me as a teacher, but I beg of you, please do not take any more of my family members. I beg of you." My answer came back, loud and clear.

"You need to do one thing. First, write me a thank-you letter." *For what?* I thought, but I did.

I thanked God for all the lessons I was about to receive and have already received in my life, and I promised I would continue on in gratitude, which has become a gift I love to give. Well, when it came time for mastectomies, a great surgeon and plastic surgeon were sent to me. I did all pre-work ups with the plastic surgeon I had chosen, and, after a few appointments, I could never get into see this plastic surgeon.

I was set up with another surgeon—a female plastic surgeon—who had been chosen for me, along with her nurse. I tried many times to get back with my first choice surgeon, but God kept sending me this female plastic surgeon. God would not allow my first choice, and I fought his decision and directions, but he knew what was best for me, even if I didn't yet!

Twelve months later, I took my secret to my father's grave. He passed away three months after being diagnosed with stomach, bladder, and prostate cancer. This would have devastated him, not one daughter but two with the same devastating disease. Yes, today I talk with him in heaven, and I tell him, "Daddy, I've really got some great people in my life." My life has been blessed by the people I have been able to experience in my life.

Today, once again I feel the pain and loss that I felt when I lost my dad. I write you this letter, with devastation in my heart, tears flowing so that I can barely see what I'm writing. Yesterday I lost my great plastic surgeon and nurse. I want you to know you made a huge impact in my life and in the lives of my family. Wow, did God know what he was doing when he sent me to you. Your compassion, concern, and persistence to do what is right for me have won me over, not to mention your artistic skills.

Many know your work before I tell them who did surgery.

I want you to know that if I may be of any help to you in the future, I would be willing to guide/teach and tell my story. Please feel free and call upon me if I can help in the works to pull another through who is facing a journey similar to my own.

As I read back through my past three years of journals, the hectic schedules—juggling work, doctors appointments (sometimes seven in a month), mammograms, ultrasounds, biopsies, chemo, radiations—left little time for mental well-being. The miracles of one person, not to mention a team of people, totally amazed me. Through all the chaos, you all made everything come together and helped get me past a difficult time in my life.

As I look back on my life before cancer, I now can say I am grateful to have experienced all I have through the course of the disease. I would not take back any of it for it has made me stronger and a greater person. Had I not gone through the journey, I would have not seen your great artistic works or the compassion of you both as you poured your hearts out trying to get me back to health. Your sessions were healing to me, both mentally and physically.

Great words you would both say as I would come to, tears flowing from my eyes. You stayed strong and let me cry so that later my tears could become laughter. My soul grew within even as my body was decaying without. You both are blessings to my curse. The magic was in my mind, but I needed your great expertise to help it grow and nourish it to achieve spiritual enlightenment.

It is both of you who helped me find my lost inner soul; you helped me find who I really was behind my makeup, hair, and clothes, but first something had to change for me to accomplish that great mission. I recognized that there is a mind within me that knows all the answers to all of my problems. The first step to finding my answers was to go within, and you both helped me do that.

Wow, what a great journey it has been with the two of you. To my nurse, you are such a beautiful, gentle, and giving person. You have more to give than I think you realize. You are so filled with love and compassion and enthusiasm; you have this infinite power to mask your fear to help strengthen others, but you also know when to be soft. You're not afraid to let down your guard and shed a tear in the silent sessions. I respect and love this about you; our great talks, hugs, tears—they all got me through. I will truly miss you. Your dad is smiling down on you—little girl, he so very proud of you and all your works and accomplishments!

To my plastic surgeon, you will be greatly missed! Behind your shy, gentle smile and great composure are a huge heart and great expertise and artistry. You are so inspiring. I admire your perseverance and courage to go the extra mile to assure the utmost satisfaction for the patient that you see as a human being and not a number. You are a book of knowledge but are always willing to learn more. You are a compassionate, strong, and giving person. You have the guts to stand up for what is best. I love your cold hands and warm heart, and I will truly miss you. Today I feel as if something inside me has died.

No gravesite to go to. No words needed to be spoken, only tears shed, feelings of sorrow, feelings of happiness; emotions run wild once again as I feel the loss of two great people, my nurse and plastic surgeon. I greatly appreciated everything you have ever done for me through this journey and would have not wanted to take this journey without you both!

Best wishes always,
Jeanne Kremers

P.S. Kitana is an artist also, she does not sew as well as my plastic surgeon yet, but she uses her skills and is a poet on paper. Today she also shows her appreciation to both of you from her heart to the paper as do I.

*To Grandma's Special Nurse:*

*To Grandma's Plastic Surgeon:*

P.P.S. The gift you both have given to me far exceeds anything I could ever say on give back to you. So today I give you something that can never be taken from me; it cannot be bought, measured, or stolen in any other way. It has to be given up willingly as I today pour out my heart to you willingly and freely as it is overflowing with joy from knowing you. You both have my highest and utmost respect and gratitude for all you do for others; you have a great team.

## A Letter to Brad

Brad,

You have grown up to be such a handsome young man, with great morals and skills; you surprise me each and every day with the things that you can do. Your meekness reminds me of me, tiptoeing around, trying not to hurt any feelings, but keeping the hurt to yourself instead. I admire your compassion but also want to tell you it's okay to share yourself with others sometimes. I see how protective you are of me and all the ones you love; what a great quality in a young man. I am so proud of the man you've become.

Enjoy your life as you know it, and make the best of every waking moment you are given, for life is a treasure that you have been given. Do not waste it with anger. Forgive, forget, and move on; it is forgiveness that the gold is to be captured.

Brad, I recognize your hardships and struggles and know you will come out on top and learn from them, as hard as I know they are and feel. Life is full of lessons, some hard and some easy; it is all in the way you perceive them. They can all be easy if you know how to ride the tide.

Trust in yourself, and never give up—your love, compassion, commitment, and dedication will always pull you through. Trust God that he will assist you always up in the best path for you; it is not always the one you believe you should take.

Love always,
Mom xoxo


## LETTER TO KIRA

Kira,

You have grown up to be such a beautiful woman. I sit back and watch you work as a mother. I may not have always mothered as I should have, but I did the best I could, and when I see you with Kitana, how you play and react together, your giggles and smiles, I realize I must have done something very right. You make me stand so proud. You have taught me so much all these years, how to love, laugh, and enjoy the little things as we know it.

Life is as hard or as easy as you make it. Enjoy every precious minute; they are all gone before we realize what has happened. Also, there is too much good in life to let the bad weigh us down, so don't waste your time being angry. It takes so much energy that could be used for happiness.

I am so proud to have been your mother and shared a big part of your life. Watching you grow up and mother your brother as I went to school for respiratory therapy, I realized then what a strong girl you were. All our walks to Bowlus every day no matter what to get you and Brad a treat, my mental vacation, your devastating breakdowns as a pre-teen (hormones do the talking), my protecting you as a mother hen, chasing your now-husband off our property—all this I cherish because it is a part of our past.

I also want you to know that I realize that you made a wise decision when you married your husband, even if I was difficult in the beginning. I see now how much you love him, and I respect all your love together. He is an awesome father to Kitana. It makes me laugh and fills my heart with joy and happy tears as I watch him now. Kira, know I never meant to hurt you, only to protect you always.

I am so proud of who you turned out to be.

Love always,
Mom, XOXO

## LETTER TO DUANE

Two things in life that matter in the end to me:

1. Family and friends
2. The love you give and have given.

Duane, you have been such a treasure that has been given to me. I am so grateful for the time God has given me to share with you. We have had tough times, but I would not have wanted to experience those times with anyone else. I love your enthusiasm for life and your always-positive attitude—the way you make things work out even if you have no idea how it will look.

I treasure our time together. When it's just the two of us, there are no words needed, just holding hands, tears, and hugs. At times I lie awake watching you sleep and think about how we are bound at our hearts. We don't always need words to communicate; just a look in your eyes, the window to your soul, tells it all.

You are such a kind, gentle man. I hit the lottery when we decided to share our lives together. I do not regret, not for one second, any of the life we have shared together.

Although it's been a difficult few years, I believe that all the trials we have faced came into our lives for a reason, and someday all the pieces will fall into place and we'll realize why we had to learn so many lessons.

Never give up on who you are, for you are part of why I am who I am.

Proud to be your wife.

Love always,
Jeanne

## LETTER TO KITANA

Dear Kitana, my sweet little monkey-shine,

Your little body is only three years old, but you have the mind of a compassionate, caring grandma. My sweet, little monkey-shine, you are so gentle and kindhearted. My heart is so filled with joy as my body and mind are exhausted. As I struggle to keep going, you are my little caretaker, always here to help me. You are so nonjudgmental; you don't see the devastation and all that I lack right now. You only see love.

Some day you will grow up and make your parents as proud as you have already made Papa Cheech and me in such a short period of time. I sometimes feel like I robbed you of your fun times with Grandma, but I will forever be grateful that I have those tiny hands and their healing touch next to me as I walk this journey and fight the monster (cancer).

I will always treasure our time together—the head paintings and crafty thank-you letters that were encouraged by you; the butterfly kisses that tickle my eyes; waking up as you climb into my bed to snuggle with me, knowing I'm too sick to play with you. I will carry with me always the memories of waking up on my good days as you force me to put my feet on the floor and shower me with snuggles and kisses; going on secret hunts to catch the perfect butterfly—those adventures force me to go outside and take a breath of fresh air. I love the great fun of hours upon hours of playing dress-up and getting a special fashion show—hearing the great announcement of who I'm seeing walk the "runway" sporting different wigs that I'm supposed to wear instead of you, but I was too afraid. You have made it so easy for me to cope.

Mostly I will miss the kisses from my heart to yours. These are truly the very best of all the kisses. You have taught me so much. How to live with nothing but have everything I could possibly need.

I love you so much, monkey-shine.

Love, Grandma Cheech

## LETTER TO MY FUTURE GRANDCHILDREN

To my future grandbabies,

I sit here and wonder about you a lot. I wonder what Kira and Bradley will call you. Are you a Charlie, a Mason, a Lilly, or an Ella? Will you inherit that beautiful red hair from your mom and carry on the trait? Or will my beautiful red-headed grandchild be the niece, not daughter, to my own beautiful redhead daughter? Perhaps you'll have hair like your dad, my Bradley—starting out blond and turning to dark brown over the years. Or will he be your uncle Bradley?

I can hear your giggles echo throughout the house as we play hide-and-seek, but I can never find you, even though you hide in the same spot time after time. I hear your cries, and I want to pick you up, comfort you, and rock you until you feel safe, as I have a gift for soothing grandchildren—grandmas do this best.

I wonder what your personality is like; will it be strong or shy? I wonder who you look like, mom or dad, auntie or uncle. I want to catch frogs, worms, and grasshoppers with you, to play dress-up and make forts out of the kitchen chairs and tables as I did so many times with Kitana. I want to help you catch your very own butterfly and watch you feed it sugar water on a cotton ball and to hear what silly little name you chose for it and watch you care for it as your first pet. I want to take you for walks and bike rides. I want to teach you the alphabet and what sounds all the letters make—"G" is for "grandma" and "L" is for "love." I want to be there to hear about your first love and see you marry your best friend. I want to see your children.

I want to promise to keep you safe and keep the loving bond of Grandma Cheech, for I will always be with you, even though it may only be in your heart. For today I can tell you that I have loved you for such a long time—long before your mom and dad even knew you.

I imagined you and saw you deep within my heart long before you were born.

It is with a heavy heart that I write you this letter, for right now that is all you are, a wish and a dream of mine. And all I can offer for now is this, the hopes and wants that I have for you. You are my driving force to push forward every day, even when I feel like I don't have an ounce left to give. Know that I will always love you and you will always have a special spot within my heart.

My deepest love,
Grandma Cheech


## A Thank You from All of Us

Life is full of changes, and not every day can be paradise. Together as a family we've faced reality, the day-to-day "bumps in the road" that test every family's patience. We've been in many challenging situations, and the miracle is when we thought it was impossible, friends, cow-orkers, and family help out and show us that our "big challenges" become much less with such great support. We just want to extend out greatest appreciation toward all of you that have touched our lives with your greatness and generosity.

I leave you with this. I love to laugh; it is so healing emotionally. It takes so much more energy to be angry or sad than it does to be happy and excited in life. I choose now at this moment to lift my head and be happy and wear this disease as if I had a lesson for people. I will wear it with elegance and grace, like none have before. I will glow with radiance from within, for that glow was there all the time. I just needed to let people see the real me, stripped down, not hiding a thing. My soul, my beautiful soul is about to shine.

Follow me to get current updates:
www.facebook.com/JeanneKremersTheChosenOne